Adventures of a F

Adventures of a Footloose Hippie

George M. Eberhart

BURNINGDAYLIGHT

COLORADO

The prose in this book is a work of nonfiction.

Library of Congress Control Number: 2024930390
Eberhart, George M. 1950–
Adventures of a Footloose Hippie
ISBN 978-1-735-7731-8-6

Cover design by Megan Ryan

First Edition
Printed in the United States of America

B U R N I N G D A Y L I G H T, Fort Collins, Colorado, an imprint of Pearn and Associates, Inc.

Dedication

This book is dedicated to my traveling companions Jim and Steve, Geoff, Dave, Ron, Gog, Frank, Tom, and Sally, and to my hosts Karl, Hans Eugen, Frau Affolter, Tim, and Ollie.

Also by George M. Eberhart

A Survey of Ufologists and Their Use of the Library (1978)

A Geo-Bibliography of Anomalies (1980)

Monsters: A Guide to Information on Unaccounted For Creatures (1983)

UFOs and the Extraterrestrial Contact Movement: A Bibliography (1986)

The Roswell Report: A Historical Perspective (1991)

The Whole Library Handbook, 5 editions (1991–2013)

Mysterious Creatures: A Guide to Cryptozoology (2002)

The Librarian's Book of Lists (2010)

Table of Contents

Introduction

It was 1971.

In January, Senator George McGovern launched his campaign for the US presidency, one year before the first Democratic primaries. In February, the Apollo 14 astronauts landed on the Moon and returned safely. In March, Led Zeppelin performed "Stairway to Heaven" publicly for the first time. In April, some 200,000 people protested the Vietnam War on the Mall in Washington, D.C. In May, National Public Radio broadcast its "All Things Considered" program for the first time. On June 13, the *New York Times* began publishing the Pentagon Papers.

Meanwhile, I was living in Columbus, Ohio, and attending Ohio State University (OSU) as an undergraduate. I had been taking classes nearly continuously since I graduated from Watterson High School in June 1968 (with time out for a couple of adventures, as you will see). I hadn't decided on a major yet, and I was focusing on all the required courses before deciding on history, journalism, or even some kind of science.

In 1970, I had taken a night job as a male attendant at Riverside Methodist Hospital to help pay for college costs. It was an opportunity to observe the workings of the US hospital system, even though the duties were sometimes sad—taking care of bedpan accidents, turning immobile patients on their sides, moving patients in wheelchairs or gurneys to get therapy or an operation, restraining patients in the psychiatric ward when they were receiving shock treatments (yes, they still did that), and wrapping up the bodies of patients who had passed (including my one VIP, famed golfer Jack Nicklaus's father, Charlie Nicklaus). And the night shift was often quiet, so there was ample time to study or complete homework.

The hospital administration was rather strict, but I soon discovered they could be flexible when confronted with reality. When I took the job, they had a firm employee grooming policy that prohibited any male facial hair. In the interview, they asked me why I was sporting a mustache and goatee. They probably expected some answer like "because I want to be free, man." However, I regaled them with my love for the literature of classical Greece, whose philosophers and poets sprouted beards of some kind. They thought that was admirable, but I still had to shave to get the job because, they thought, facial hair would upset their elderly, conservative patients.

Some months after I was hired, I conspired with another male attendant to write a petition that protested the policy. It was a lengthy document. My colleague had a taste for the law, so he wrote up a critique based on local, state, and federal statutes and court cases. My portion centered on the history of Methodism and how many of the prominent Methodists of the 19th century were elegantly bewhiskered. I included many illustrations and even invoked some biblical precedents. The petition worked. Success! We were granted the right to grow our facial hair back, and I've had either a beard or mustache almost ever since (except for a couple weeks in early 1992 when I had a gig as an extra in the *Hoffa* film starring Jack Nicholson).

The hospital job was intriguing enough that I thought I might continue as a healthcare worker or technician of some kind. However, in early 1971 a crackdown took place and our job duties expanded so that little study time remained. I had to give up the job and go back to studying full-time.

It occurred to me that perhaps I should take some time off from classes and try to figure out what my major should be. A 20-minute interview with someone in the OSU History Department soon convinced me that, although I have always loved the topic, I did not want to wind up as a high school history teacher. That sounded like a nightmare, as I preferred to do research.

Then I ran across a classified advertisement in the student newspaper offering an opportunity to "live and work abroad." The Anglo-America Association would arrange for your transportation to England and set you up with employers who were eager to hire help for the summer. I contacted them, and they seemed to be a reputable organization. The initial cost for the flight over there was reasonable, and I reckoned that, with my experience, I might even be able to get some kind of job at a hospital. Then, when my duties were over, I could go to the Continent and visit my cousin Karl Johé in Germany and my friend Dave Hall, who was stationed somewhere in Europe at a US Army base.

And that is what launched my great European adventure. It did not turn out the way I had anticipated, but through both initiative and happenstance I was able to re-engineer it into an experience somewhat like the Grand Tour that upper-class students of the 19th century embarked on as part of their aristocratic education. The itinerary encompassed England, Scotland, Wales, Germany, France, Spain, and Switzerland—but not the usual ports of call. For example, I spent five days as an official monster hunter at Loch Ness.

I had been in the habit of keeping a somewhat exaggerated diary of my major trips. Two of them are reproduced here after "Adventure in Europe, 1971," the primary narrative—"The Big Trek, 1969," the story of a hitchhike across the US; and "The Long Haul, 1970," a narrative of a car trip with a co-worker of mine to California.

So, in preparation for visiting England in 1971, I bought a small, six-ring notebook for the specific purpose of keeping a record of my travels. And indeed I did, taking notes in longhand for two-and-a-half months. I had intended to convert this into a formal narrative for entertainment purposes while my memory of the adventure was still fresh, fleshing out details as needed. And I managed to do this and type it up upon my return for the first five days of the trip. But this project was nipped in the bud when shortly after my return I declared a journalism major and got very busy with classes again—in hindsight, probably as much a result of recording the events of the trip as my rationalization that, as a journalist, I could write articles about history and science and the paranormal, three of my lifelong interests.

The notebook languished in a box of memoirs for the next 52 years—through two marriages, a bachelor's degree in journalism, a master's degree in librarianship, a job as a law librarian at the University of Kansas, and many years as an editor at the American Library Association in Chicago. I had taken it out occasionally but never read it straight through, deterred by the unruly scrawl of my rushed handwriting.

In February 2023, for some reason, I decided it was time to preserve the narrative by putting it into a digital format. In the course of reading and processing it, I discovered many things that I had long forgotten, and I was struck by the way that it captured the flavor of a generation of people and places and practices and philosophies that no longer exist.

In fact, I learned that I have not changed that much over the past 50+ years, except perhaps in being more cautious and less intense. Some people find their youthful selves to be an embarrassment or completely alien. For the most part (but definitely not 100%), I recognize my 21-year-old self as someone with the same interests, preoccupations, and personality quirks that I have today—including a propensity for exaggeration with an intent to both amuse and confuse.

A digital diary could also be shared with my cousin Karl and two of the people who accompanied me on the trip and who now were Facebook friends. I was gratified by their positive responses, so I sent it to another friend, Victor Pearn, when I was helping him copyedit his autobiography, *Swinging Away*. He suggested that Pearn and Associates publish it as a memoir that resonates with the spirit of a bygone era. I hope you enjoy it as well!

Just a few more words of explanation. I do characterize myself here as a "hippie," which was true, as I had adopted a somewhat countercultural lifestyle in response to the Vietnam War and the influences of rock music. However, we usually referred to ourselves as "longhairs" or "freaks," while other people, outsiders, referred to us as hippies. Yet "hippies" has persisted, and the other terms have not.

I had no problems smoking marijuana, as most of my friends did too, and that extended to this trip as well. The amount of hashish consumed at US army bases was astounding.

I apparently consumed large quantities of beer and wine as well. My excuse is that I had just turned 21, and the contrast in quality between American beer and wine (think Pabst Blue Ribbon and Mogen David 20/20) and European beer and wine at the time was breathtaking.

In some places my characterization of police officers is unfavorable. I can only say that in those days, certain law enforcement officers singled out long-haired, hippie-looking types for harassment in the hopes of making a bust for possession of a controlled substance. This was the case in Columbus, Ohio, especially in college bars frequented by freaks. Police might enter the establishment, detain individuals as "suspects," or even arrest them under some pretense and frisk them for weed. Though not as serious as the "driving while black" profiling in effect both then and now, it certainly affected contemporary countercultural attitudes.

The raw diary that I kept has been edited moderately and enhanced with some background and commentary on the places I visited. However, some things I just do not remember at all, so if you are wondering what I meant when I called Kate a "hell-nymph," I too am at a loss to explain. I'm sure it was significant at the time.

As for people mentioned in the text, Geoff Reed and Dave Hall have had a chance to read the entries, but the Kohl brothers (a pseudonym) have not. I lost track of them a long time ago, but I don't think I've said anything in here that they would have disagreed with at the time. I have also lost track of Frank (in "The Big Trek") and Tom and Sally (in "The Long Haul") as well.

A handful of brief quotations from Andrew Sinclair's book *Gog* (Macmillan, 1967) accompany appropriate parts of the text.

I do apologize if there are any inaccuracies in my account or any unintended inferences.

Adventure in Europe, 1971

Thursday, June 24, 1971

It all started in the wee hours. The night was cool and gusty. The pallid full moon scowled at the lonely house at 357 West Second Avenue in Columbus, Ohio, where I lay dozing. It was an inexpensive rental apartment where I had been living for about a year just to the south of Ohio State University, within walking distance of classes.

Jim and Steve, the Kohl boys, were supposed to come around and pick me up to go to the bus station where we would all catch our bus for New York City. I had never met Jim or Steve before except over the phone—a singular coincidence, actually. Before last week I was planning to go see Europe by myself, companionless in an alien land. But when I called up the Switchboard, a community services center in Columbus, to try to sell my car, the guy who answered happened to mention that he was going to England with the Anglo-America Association, the very organization that was providing my own transportation to that mystic isle and that was supposed to get me a summer job somewhere when I arrived. This Switchboard guy was Jim Kohl, and after chatting awhile we decided to go to Europe together, as both Jim and his brother Steve hoped to find jobs there as well.

As I lay waiting for the Kohls to arrive, I pondered the life I would lead in England—it would be so different from Columbus with its pressures and pollution and police. Perhaps I would never come back! Maybe I would find a small cottage in Northumberland and live the rest of my life tending sheep or growing clover.

At 2:30 a.m., the Kohls arrived. Steve came to the door: He was a flaxen-haired lad who wore braces that peeped through an affable grin. He thrust his lank 6-feet-2-inch frame inside the screen door and lisped, "You must be George." I replied that I was, or at least that's what people told me, then I let him in, and we carried my gear out to the car where Jim and his parents were waiting. Jim was a mild-mannered, introspective type of fellow who got quite neurotically nervous about the most trivial things. Right now, he was nervous about going to England, which might have been justified, except that he'd been to Europe before and worked as a dishwasher in a Paris café. I discovered the reason for Jim's neurosis when I met Mrs. Kohl—she was the overly protective type who didn't want her boys to get into any sort of predicament whatsoever. During the whole ride to the bus station, she rambled on about how worried she was that the Anglo-America Association was a nasty organization and that we would all get stranded in London and run out of money, and she kept reminding Steve and Jim to brush their teeth and wash behind their ears and eat well and wear their rubbers, etc. All they could do was answer sheepishly, "Yes, Mum." Mr. Kohl was a Bulgarian immigrant; he didn't say too much of anything—he just drove.

Somehow we made it to the Greyhound station, where we were about an hour early. Jim and Steve said prolonged goodbyes to Mom and Dad while I paced excitedly. Our bus left at 3:30 and we were on our way into the Unknown. Goodbye and good riddance, Columbus—farewell, City of Inertia!

There was some weird guy who got on the bus with us who was taking photographs of the passengers and the undersides of overpasses. He must have been an out-of-work journalist. Jim and I rapped and got to know each other, then slept off and on. Around 5:00 a.m., we wheeled through Wheeling, West Virginia, and ate some chicken that Maril (my roommate's girlfriend) had fixed for us before we left. At 7:00 we arrived at Pittsburgh, Pennsylvania, where we had a "35 minute" stop for 50 minutes; we bought some expensive coffee and waited on the bus, listening to some old lady talking about her daughter who was in Vienna. By the time we got going again it was 8:00 a.m. and Pittsburgh was smack in the middle of a traffic jam. The driver inched his way through that, then zoomed back onto the freeway to Breezewood, Pennsylvania, where we had another rest stop at 10:45. Steve and especially Jim were still all fried out about getting a job; at the most fleeting mention of our uncertain future, Jim would gnash his teeth and groan about how the future oppressed him.

7

At 2:00 p.m., we rolled into Philadelphia, Pennsylvania, suffering from sheer exhaustion. We'd been on the road for almost 12 hours and our gluteus muscles were beginning to realize it. Why we didn't take a plane to New York, I don't know, except that Mrs. Kohl felt it would be safer to take a bus—we wouldn't get as confused on a bus as we would on a plane, I think her reasoning went. In Philly we changed buses and sped into New Jersey, a flat, muggy floodplain with too many people on it. We passed an odd structure that looked like a gigantic volleyball resting on a smooth cracker box—according to a sign, it belonged to the US Air Force Project Spacetrack Aerospace Defense Command, an early effort to detect artificial satellites and space probes, both domestic and foreign. The project was headquartered in Colorado Springs, but this must have been a substation.

At 4:00 p.m., we saw in the smoggy distance the hazy relief of the Manhattan skyline—the same one you used to see E. G. Marshall stand in front of all the time on *The Defenders* TV series. The tumult and confusion of New York City life swarmed about us: cab drivers, drunks, perverts, WASPs, WASCs, WASJs, and Black Americans all ran about knocking into each other, intentionally and unintentionally. New York certainly has the best and the worst of everything known to man.

Twenty minutes later, we pulled into the terminal and crawled off the bus we had been living on for the past 13 hours, dragging our gear behind us. Jim and Steve just stood around worrying, so I had to be the dominant male figure of the group and lead the way to the information booth, which lay behind a nebulous mass of desks and humanity. The nice man at the booth said we could go to John F. Kennedy International Airport by either subway, bus, or taxi. Both subway and bus seemed rather confusing, especially since I had never been to New York before, and I just knew that it would be murder trying to take either one at 5:00 p.m. rush hour carrying backpacks and sleeping bags. On the bus we'd get lost and on the subway we'd get mugged and lost. So after a heated debate, we decided to take a taxi. I'd heard that the one thing I should do if I ever got to New York was to take a taxi. I talked Jim and Steve into it, and we found one outside, driven by a gaunt Puerto Rican who tossed us a *Life* magazine to read as we got in his cab. Little did I know what we were in for.

We narrowly escaped death at every turn. The Puerto Rican would squeeze his cab into the tiniest spaces available, honking his horn continually. Whenever another car would try to pull in front of him, he would launch into a torrent of verbal defamation in colloquial Spanish, uttering peculiar grunts of disgust and making wild, frustrated gestures in between vile curses. The traffic was so bad that it took us a whole hour to get from the bus station to Kennedy, but it was worth it. It was a thrill a minute. We got out at the Northeast Airlines terminal (Terminal 2) at 5:45 p.m., paying the cabbie $14 for our transportation and entertainment.

The clerk at the ticket counter told us that we had to wait until 9:00 p.m. when someone important, a representative from Notre Dame University, would arrive. All the Anglo-America Association people were traveling on a Notre Dame charter flight on Caledonian Airways.

The three of us checked our luggage at a nearby locker and wandered off to buy hot dogs and sandwiches at a New York rip-off snack bar where the beers cost 85 cents. We couldn't do much but sit around and wait because the airport was too far away from anything for it to be worthwhile to go sightseeing. Jim sat around brooding while Steve and I amused ourselves by exploring a flight of stairs which we thought might lead to an observation deck. We were wrong—they led to a dead end, and we turned back, cursing man's vanity.

At long last, 8:30 p.m. rolled around and we got in line at the ticket counter, managing to salvage second place. While we were waiting, we talked to other people and found only maybe one or two others from Anglo-America—everyone else was from Notre Dame, Boston, South Carolina, the International Students Association, and other places. We were all a bit worried about our flight status, still not knowing whether or not Anglo-America had swindled us. But at 9:00 p.m., the Notre Dame representative arrived, and we found our names on his list; he gave us our tickets, we paid a $10 surcharge, got our baggage checked, pulled out our wallets again, and paid an $8 head tax—not because we were acid heads, but because the US wanted to squeeze more money out of our pockets.

The nice Caledonian stewardess lady told us we had to get in line again to talk to the Notre Dame man because we needed to be assigned a seat number. She also mentioned our flight had been delayed until 4:00 a.m. (it was originally scheduled for 11:00 p.m.), but she said we would all get a free meal at some airport hotel, courtesy of Caledonian. While I waited in line again, Steve and Jim scampered off to a phone booth to call their parents, who were nice enough to contact my dad and tell him we were going to be all right. In line I met an old friend of my high-school friend Ned's, Kris Gilpin, who was going to England through Anglo-America. The last time I'd seen Kris was just before she and Ned were inadvertently arrested for curfew violation during the Ohio State University student protests in late April 1970—just before the more infamous Kent State University demonstrations that led to the shooting deaths of four students. Afterward, she'd absconded to Israel to live in a kibbutz for a while. Now she was off again to live in Amsterdam, and she gave us her phone number there and said to come visit her for a week or so if we were down that way. She was traveling with a friend named Margaret.

Finally, we learned that we didn't need a seat number after all, so we just wandered around until 11:00 p.m. when the buses came to take us to our free meal. When we went outside, the polluted urban air stung our eyes and they began to water. The Black bus driver, a friendly chap, said that New Yorkers got used to it all and really couldn't breathe any other kind of air. The airport hotel, which was possibly the Idlewild Arms, was just down the road, and when we got there we were treated to a sumptuous meal of fried chicken and potatoes, which Steve wolfed down with amazing relish. He also had a gin and 7-Up. This was a real treat for Steve, who was just a youngster of 19, eager for any legal chance to imbibe spiritous liquors. We began talking to a young lady named Mary from Boston and a guy from South Carolina named Bill. We discussed Boston, skiing, religion, and esoteric philosophy.

After dinner we went out to the lobby. This was a moderately swank hotel—there was a heated swimming pool in the back with all kinds of exotic plants growing around it—a veritable jungle. Kris got out a set of jacks and a luminous yo-yo, which we all did tricks with until we began to become weary of children's games. Our buses didn't leave until 2:30 a.m. for some reason or other. By this time, the three of us were ready to say our lay-me-downs right in the airport, since we had been awake more or less continuously for the past 25 hours.

Nothing to do at Kennedy but sit around and talk to Mary from Boston, who invited us to Ireland if we ever got there. The airport was completely dead, and so was everyone waiting for the flight to leave; if, indeed, it would ever leave. There was another line to wait in at the gate as 4:00 a.m. got closer. Finally, a pert little Scottish stewardess admitted us to the airplane, after first letting on a couple with a tired little boy in their arms. Steve, Jim, and I found seats with a decent view, got our gear and tickets straightened out, and girt our loins for the exotic adventures to come. This was it. We were on our way to a new continent.

Friday, June 25, 1971

The plane trip took 6½ hours. This was Steve's first time in a jet, so we let him have the window seat. He was quite fascinated by the infinite variety of clouds we passed by, and he wondered aloud at the otherworldliness of the sights of the upper atmosphere. Jim and I, both seasoned jet passengers, smiled knowingly at each other. Before long it was daylight again and the clouds dispersed so that we could see the land below us. We observed what we thought was Prince Edward Island, Canada, and offshore we could see tiny boats churning across the shining waters. Pretty soon we were well over the Atlantic Ocean and the scenery got dull again, so we took advantage of the boredom to catch up on all our lost sleep.

It was a lot easier sleeping on the plane than on the bus because there was less noise, and the drone of the engines acted as a hypnotic lullaby. The Scottish steward and stewardesses woke us up for breakfast, and later they served us a snack of typical airplane-type food. We ripped off some salt, sandwiches, and some

11

plastic eating utensils, in case we should need them in the future. Jim was going out of his mind with worry—he frittered and fizzled about what we would do when we got to England, what would happen to us if we got stranded, what the chances were that a meteorite would hit the plane and we would all be killed, etc. I went back to sleep.

Later that afternoon, Merrie Olde England hove into view. The pilot flew low over the Sussex countryside and announced that we were approaching Gatwick Aerodrome from the east. The scenery was beautiful from the air—we saw all sorts of quaint little hamlets, country houses, and countless patterns of yellow and green fields separated by hedgerows. We zoomed over narrow country lanes and buzzed the funny English cars below us. Then Gatwick loomed up, a sprawling concrete jellyfish in a green and yellow sea. Our hearts were in our mouths as we landed. What lay in store for us when we disembarked? What fantastic adventures were fated to happen to us? What on earth is a foreign country like?

"Well, here we are in a foreign country," I winced as the plane's wheels ground to a halt. It was 3:45 p.m. We looked outside the window and the first Englishmen we saw were white-suited airport attendants. "Wow, there *are* people living here," Steve observed. We got off the plane and strolled down a long corridor toward Customs. My God, another line. We were speechless. What do you say when you can't tell if you're dreaming or not? England. I rolled the word around on my tongue, tasting the syllables. Now that I'm here, what do I do with it? I mused.

We finally got to the customs man, who asked me how much money I had and how long I was going to stay in his country spending it. I told him I had 400 sound American dollars that I would flagrantly squander on frivolous British trinkets and souvenirs. The man scowled and stamped my passport. Jim also had no trouble going through.

But Steve was a different story. The customs man hassled him about having only $150 and asked him how he expected to live on that for two months. "You wooldn't be thinkin' o' findin' work 'ere, now would ye?" he sneered. "But— I— I—" Steve stammered. "At's wot I thawt," the customs man said, stamping Steve's passport with a special stamp limiting Steve's stay to two months and specifying that he could not work while he was staying here.

Anglo-America had warned us not to tell the customs people that we were planning to get jobs, because the Ministry of Labour was paranoid about foreigners coming in and getting employed instead of able-bodied Englishmen. There was nothing we could do about it now except wait until we saw the Anglo-America people.

After going through Customs, we were officially on British soil. Our first deed was to go to the bank at the aerodrome and convert some traveler's checks into pounds; thus we obtained the proper currency for using the pay telephones. These phones were a complete enigma at first. I wanted to call Anglo-America, headquartered on the Isle of Wight, which from Gatwick was long distance.

You have to dial direct—none of this letting the operator do all the work like in America. First you dial the number, and then you wait until it rings and someone answers, then you lickety-split cram a 10-pence (10p) piece into the machine so you won't be disconnected. After that, you have to stuff 2p and 10p coins into the slot at intervals of a minute or so. Needless to say, it took me a half hour to learn all this, especially since two out of the three available phones were out of order and not marked as such, but a friendly Englishman took pains to explain the complicated process to me. By the time I got hold of Anglo-America, I had lost about 15p in the blasted phones from abortive attempts at communication, and I didn't have enough change or energy left to talk for more than 30 seconds, so I said to hell with it, Jim, let's get a train ticket to Portsmouth and worry about it there.

We chose Portsmouth, a port city in Hampshire on the south coast, because there was a ferry there that would take us to the Isle of Wight. Our train tickets cost £1/10 (one pound, 10 shillings). Decimalization had just come to Britain in February of this year, but many places were still using shillings, in addition to the new pence coins, and even the locals seemed a bit confused.

We didn't have to go to a train station because there was one right there at the aerodrome. Gatwick is way in the middle of the country on the border between Surrey and Sussex and, although it's supposed to be a London airport, it's a good 29 miles away from London. That's why it has a train station.

The phones were confusing, but the trains were worse. We must have asked five different conductors and 20 innocent bystanders whether this was the right platform, whether this was the train to Portsmouth, and so on. Finally, we piled onto the Portsmouth train at 5:10 p.m. and stumbled to a seat, fidgeting nervously, not having the faintest idea what we were doing. The train was crowded with British businessmen, stolidly reading the *Evening Standard,* pretending not to notice as we bumped into them or gawked naively at the scenery.

The scenery *was* nice, though. Quaint little country manors were scattered here and there across the countryside, masked by hedgerows and herds of Guernsey cattle. It was mostly flattish farm country, since this was the south of England. We anxiously consulted our road map every time the train made a stop, to see whether we were in Portsmouth yet. At last, a conductor came along to check our tickets, and he told us we'd have to change trains in Littlehampton, a stop along the English Channel in West Sussex. After a while, we crossed the chalky South Downs and came to the seacoast and pulled into Littlehampton, where we just barely managed to find the Portsmouth train. This second train was much better because we found a semi-private compartment where we could lounge more freely and discuss our plans.

When we were waiting for the train at Gatwick, I had run across another confused American who had a youth hostel handbook with him. The book listed one hostel in Portsmouth located at a place called Cosham. I figured our best bet was to head there first and see if we could get a place to stay. We pulled into Portsmouth station around 6:25 p.m. and asked the information man how to get to the Cosham hostel. He told us we'd have to catch a green bus north and we'd eventually get there. Later on, we discovered that red buses were for short rides within the city, while green buses were for longer rides to suburbs and other towns. Cosham was a whole different town, but it was only a bit north of

Portsmouth. Had we known where Cosham was prior to this, we might've gotten off the train there, since it was only one or two stops before the main Portsmouth station.

After consoling Jim and Steve and telling them everything would be all right, I found a green bus with the help of a friendly little old man who took pity on us. The green bus was a standard British double decker that used (logically) a graduated fare rate depending on how far you had to go (not like Columbus Transit Company, which charged you 40 cents to go two blocks). We only paid 6p. The stops on this route weren't marked very well and the driver never called them out, but some inhabitants helped us get where we wanted to get off, namely Cosham Post Office.

We walked up Wymering Lane looking for the hostel. This is when I discovered how naturally soft-spoken Europeans tend to be—passersby gave us odd looks when they passed by us, not particularly because we looked American, but because Jim and Steve were bickering (as I then realized) pretty loudly. It wouldn't have been too noticeable in America, but it certainly was noticeable here. The surest sign of an American is his big mouth.

We found the hostel—it was beside a small church. The place looked pleasant; it was really just a big house in a more or less suburban area, but quaint. Unfortunately, the hostel manager explained that the house was all filled up, but he advised finding a Bed and Breakfast down by the Dockyard near the Isle of Wight ferry. Down there, he said, we're bound to find an inexpensive place to stay.

So we trekked back to the bus stop, just missing our bus. We had to wait another 30 minutes for the next one. This time we took the red bus marked "Dockyard," and traveled pretty much the same route we had come for another 6 pence. We noticed a lot of young people while riding the buses—the guys were invariably well-dressed, even the longhair types. If they weren't wearing a sport coat, they at least had a sharp-looking sweater and tie, a natty overcoat, and exquisitely polished shoes. There were no blue jeans, tennis shoes, or shorts for miles around, except on Americans.

When we arrived at Her Majesty's Royal Navy Dockyard, it was getting toward 9:00 p.m., but it still wasn't dark yet. Their days certainly are long here in the summer. It's because

Portsmouth is at a higher latitude (50° 48′ N) than anywhere else in the US except Alaska, just a bit farther north than Regina, Saskatchewan. In fact, the entire UK is farther north than the top of Minnesota.

Jim was getting worried because we hadn't found a place to stay, but I reassured him that there were thousands of cheap hotels waiting anxiously to clasp us to their hospitable bosoms. We wandered into an expensive hotel and quickly wandered out again, but not before getting a tip or two on cheaper places to stay. We were told that there was a Bed and Breakfast around the corner across from the "multi-story," meaning a high-rise. And if we couldn't find that, there was the Sally Port Hotel a short way down the road. We strolled around looking for the Bed and Breakfast but couldn't find it, primarily because we didn't know what a Bed and Breakfast looked like. At that time, we weren't even sure what a multi-story was either. So we gave up on that tip and went in quest of the Sally Port. The name kind of appealed to me anyway, because it reminded me of a sometime girlfriend, Psilocybin Sally (see "The Long Haul, 1970").

The three of us walked to a British Petrol (BP) station and asked the lady attendant where the Sally Port Hotel was. (Lady petrol jockeys are common in Europe—for some reason women's liberation got a head start here.) She told us to keep walking on the same road, it was just down a few blocks. So we walked and walked, Jim and Steve grumbling at each weary step, complaining about being cold and tired and hungry; but I urged them on with a hearty laugh and a good-humored slap on the back.

There it was at last: the Sally Port! The building is still there at 57–58 High Street, though in 2023 it is now just a pub and an antique store. They don't make hotels in America like they made the Sally Port. It was a vintage British hotel built in probably the 18th century—the records are unclear—but I fantasized that it might have been as old as 1525, when King Henry VIII began fooling around with Anne Boleyn in a back room at the Star Chamber when nobody else was around. Generals, admirals, and assorted aristocrats used to lounge about in the lobby, according to several plaques and certificates that hung on the wall. Most of the furniture looked to be 18th century and in good condition. All of this convinced us that we should stay there; besides, it was late, we were tired from walking such a long way, and we felt we deserved a treat. We paid the clerk £2.30 apiece. This was rather stiff, but it wasn't as bad as the other hotel we had tried.

Our room was up a winding staircase on the third floor. It had three nice bouncy beds in it with a soft blanket and spread. No doubt some 18th-century chancellor of the exchequer had spent the night here with his mistress instead of brushing up on his Magna Carta so he could advocate for a reform bill. Steve and I plopped our stuff down on the nearest beds, but Jim spread his sleeping bag on the floor because, he said, he slept more comfortably that way. Then he muttered something obscure about yoga. Steve and I were satisfied with our beds, though.

Now that we had a place to sleep, our next problem was satiating our wanton hunger. We skipped downstairs to the plush dining room, but there was no one there except for a middle-aged couple who weren't eating. We sat there for maybe 15 minutes, but as nobody came to take our order, we came to the logical conclusion that dinner was over. At places like this, the British require you to be on time for your meals, otherwise you lose out. Very punctual people, these British.

We went back upstairs to wash up. Jim went down to the bathroom first—it was on the second floor—and came back complaining that he had to relieve himself in total darkness because there was no light switch. I told him not to talk absolute rubbish, that there had to be a light switch somewhere. So I went downstairs, searched in vain for a light switch, and went to the bathroom in the dark. Later, at a more leisurely pace, I strolled into the adjacent washroom and found switches for both rooms there. Concomitantly, I discovered that Europeans generally have separate rooms for the bathtub and the toilet—thus in a large family, one can enjoy the primeval pleasures of wallowing in the bathtub for hours on end without inconveniencing anyone else.

Jim wasn't too hungry, but Steve and I were, so we went next door to our first pub—Monck's Bar. It was rather crowded, and there was nowhere to sit, but the proprietress brought out an extra bar stool for us.

To see what it would be like, I ordered a beer. The British like to drink their beer lukewarm or at room temperature; this is partly because it's traditional, partly because the weather is so abominably cold here, but mostly because beer loses quite a bit of its "flavour" if it's chilled. This was totally too much for Steve who, as I mentioned before, was only a youngster of 19 and just beginning to tackle American beers.

Steve claimed he had a delicate stomach and could only eat and drink certain things or else he'd be sick. This is what comes of being pampered. So he ordered a chilled lager, which turned out to be nothing more than a good old Carling Black Label from Canada. Then came our food, spaghetti, served by a 35-ish pub maid with a gold wig, plump thighs, and a black semi-miniskirt. Steve started talking to her in a loud voice about America and the merits of cold beer; I pretended not to notice the annoyed stares we got from fellow customers. We paid the bar lady 60p apiece, then ambled back to the Sally Port where Jim was lying in his sleeping bag writing a letter home. We wasted no time getting to sleep.

Saturday, June 26, 1971

The maid came in around 8:00 a.m. with a pot of tea for us and said that our breakfast was now being served. According to English custom, breakfast is free if you've paid for a bed—that's where the term Bed and Breakfast comes from. British food is generally unimpressive, but their breakfasts *are* filling; this one consisted of two eggs and a kind of sausage that's different from the American variety—it's not smoked and it's a bit softer. After we ate in the dining room downstairs, we packed up our luggage and asked the man at the reception desk where a cheaper place to stay was. He said that most of the students stayed at the YMCA around the corner near the seafront. Funny he didn't mention that last night before we got a room.

We found the YMCA with no trouble at all. It *was* just around the corner, possibly at 104 Penny Street—a modern, four-story, hotel-like structure wedged in between some Restoration style houses all bunched together and waiting for someone to set fire to them; across the street was an old bombed-out, 13th-century Royal Garrison Church surrounded by a gothic, Lovecraftian cemetery. We took a walk around the church while we were waiting for the YMCA proprietor to wake up at 9:00 a.m., but it was all fenced off, so we couldn't look at the epitaphs and dates on the tombstones.

Finally, the YMCA proprietor came down and we paid him £1.20 apiece for separate rooms, which is about half what we paid at the Sally Port. Of course, the furnishings weren't as luxurious and they didn't have a maid, but there was a game room with a chess board, a card table, and a foosball set that some Pakistani and Turkish fellows were forever fooling around with. We dropped our luggage off in our rooms and came downstairs to the pay phone, where we tried to get Mrs. Richardson at Anglo-America, but no one was there because it was Saturday. This set Jim off on a worry binge again, but I told him that we really couldn't do anything until Monday, and in the meantime the three of us might as well do Portsmouth up right, sightseeing-wise at least.

Our first stop was the seafront, or the harbourfront rather, which was just beyond the church—probably by the Horatio Nelson Statue or at Victoria Pier. A cold wind was blowing in from the ocean and it lashed the shore with briny kisses of seafoam. Water swirled around the blockhouse in the middle of the harbour, which was placed there to keep French and Spanish fleets from nosing around Britain's most important port. The city of Gosport loomed up on the opposite side of the harbor and, although we couldn't see it, the Isle of Wight was less than 5 miles away, across the strait. Several motorboats and a ragged sailboat or two frolicked about in the churning waters, and seagulls splashed in the offshore algae looking for minnows, sticklebacks, and other gullian delicacies.

There is something about the sea that hypnotizes a man and lures him into exploring it—Jim and I both felt it. It could be that the salt and the wind and the waves and all the activity subliminally reminded us of all those aquatic creatures our ancestors used to be—amphibians, fish, echinoderms, on down to infusoria. Life as we know it started in the sea; in fact, life may even be the sea, and the wind, and the pounding surf. But no—one has to think conventionally and believe in one God, creator of heaven and earth and all things visible and invisible, etc. A pagan concept, really. Quite unimaginative. Jim and I had some heavy thoughts then, as we gazed at Portsmouth Harbour.

Next stop was the chemist's (the British term for a non-prescription drugstore) to buy some batteries for Steve's camera. The chemist was a jovial, plump Englishman straight out of a Dickens novel who told us that if we were going sightseeing, we should see the *HMS Victory* just down the road at the Royal Navy's Docks, the *Victory* of course being the flagship of the fleet that Vice-Admiral Horatio Nelson whipped the French and Spanish navies with at the Battle of Trafalgar in 1805. He gave us explicit directions on how to get there—so explicit that it took him 20 minutes to get through it all. These English have a habit of making things twice as difficult as they really are, especially directions.

We walked down a side road, looking at all the historical plaques on the old houses that told where Duke Soandso was stabbed in a duel and General Suchandsuch seduced the Baroness of Thisandthat. After a few blocks we came to our first cathedral, Portsmouth Cathedral. It wasn't really too big or awesome, but it was there, and I felt we should acknowledge its presence by visiting it. The cathedral was erected in 1188 as a chapel dedicated to Archbishop Thomas Becket, who was murdered in Canterbury in 1170 by King Henry II's henchmen. Various archbishops added to the original structure and by 1904 it was in its present state. Inside they have a bunch of fun things like a wooden tablet showing all the famous naval engagements in which ships called *HMS Mary Rose* have taken part from 1509 to 1917; a fragment of the white ensign flown by the *HMS Victory* at Trafalgar; a 1693 pulpit surmounted by a gilded trumpeting angel; a ceramic plaque of the Madonna and Child made by Andrea della Robbia in Florence in about 1500; and the Sanctuary, which in most respects is the same as when it was first erected in 1188. We wandered around the cathedral for about 20 minutes until Jim got worried that we might be committing sacrilege by traipsing about the altar looking at things.

Down the road was the dock where the *HMS Victory* was kept. Inside the gates lay the naval ministry buildings where they had all sorts of old masts and gigantic anchors lying around for the landlubbers to marvel at. Then we came to the *Victory* herself where a tour group was just forming. It was 10p or so to go on board, a small price to pay for viewing the most famous ship of the former most powerful navy in the world.

The tour guide, a ginger-haired able-bodied seaman with a refined sense of humor, took us up on the decks to see all the points of interest. He showed us those nasty scorpions (cat-o'-nine-tails) that insubordinate sailors were flogged with, and then we were taken to the artillery rooms where the cannon peeped out of their holes to fart iron at enemy ships. We saw the men's eating quarters: sailors didn't use napkins then, of course, and all they had was a heavy piece of rope that they wiped their hands on—when the rope got really greasy, the cook scraped off all the slimy stuff and used it in his frying pan.

Or at least that's what we thought the ginger-haired seaman told us. We had a hard time understanding him because we weren't really used to British accents yet. The sound is so unusual to American ears—a ringing, lilting sort of speech—that one just tends to listen to the pleasant sounds they make without bothering about the meaning. He made a few jokes, too, which were beyond our American spheres of experience.

Then we were led to Nelson's headquarters. These were quite sumptuous indeed. Of course, he deserved it all, but aristocratic affluence is one reason why the French had a revolution. No doubt that is why Nelson was so dead set against Napoleon spreading the Revolution to other parts of Europe. In any case, Nelson died heroically at the Battle of Trafalgar on October 21, 1805. After showing us the livestock quarters and Nelson's favorite hammock, the guide showed us where Nelson actually died. It was a gloomy, stony place belowdecks where few could see him doing such an uncivilized thing. But he was courageous, committed, and charismatic, and afterward he was treated as a hero—I wish I had a nickel for every Nelson monument in England and a penny for every street sign that bears his name. The seaman showed us where Nelson took the fatal bullet, too. This was a more pleasant spot up on the top deck where he was gallantly directing the course of the battle.

While I was on deck I wanted to climb a mast or two, but the sailors wouldn't let me. They said I wasn't able-bodied enough.

After the tour, we backed away from the ship to get some pictures of it. In certain areas nearby you weren't allowed to take photos of anything, since it still was Her Majesty's Dockyard and the enemy isn't supposed to know what it looks like, I suppose.

We crossed the street and cut through pleasant Victoria Park with its animal cages filled with birds, rabbits, and guinea pigs, and its greenhouses and public footpaths, aiming for the main part of town past the Portsmouth Guildhall. On Commercial Road we nosed in all the shop windows. I bought a new roll of film in a camera shop, picked up a Top 40 pop listing (with "Indiana Wants Me" by R. Dean Taylor as Number One) in a record store, and snooped around a second-hand bookstore. Saturday is market day in Portsmouth, and we stumbled upon the outdoor market on a side street. They were selling all kinds of fruit and vegetables and fish and even some clothes and lampshades and such. Jim bought some excellent New Zealand apples which we all nibbled on until we found a small place to eat on Commercial Road—it was a hole-in-the-wall-type joint with little redeeming culinary value, but a sandwich there kept our energies up.

As we were wandering around the side streets, we were accosted by a colorful drunken fellow who claimed to be a Liverpool slummy. He walked up to us and asked if we were Irish, but Jim apologized and said, no, we're Americans. "Ahhh," he said, "just as well," and then somehow we got started talking about British politics. He was a smidgeon on the conservative side, even for an Englishman, and when he started talking about negroes, this raised Jim's ire a bit and they started arguing quietly. I threw a couple compromising comments in here and there, hoping that Jim wouldn't keep it going for so long that an international incident might develop. Nothing did, however, and the slummy gave us a heartfelt goodbye or two and lurched off down the road, his nose glowing a bright red in the afternoon sun.

After all this walking and talking we all were pretty pooped, so we walked back through Victoria Park towards the YMCA. While we were in the park, we stopped in the greenhouse to see what sort of weird, exotic vegetation they had sprouting there. We stared in awe at the profusion of tropical trees, rhododendrons, azaleas, rubber trees, and such, but the main attraction was a mynah bird that whistled loudly and uttered piercing eloquence like "Pretty birdie!" and "Your father's mustache!" all in a Cockney accent.

We went back to the harbourfront where the wind was blowing up a heavy spray that splashed up onto the path at several points. Jim and Steve and I tempted it by leaning over the stone wall and looking out over the water, but when the spray would try to get us, we would jump back quickly before we were doused. Jim got soaked once, though I believe he was secretly hoping for it. Steve took a splendid photo of the sea spray lashing Jim in the face. The spray caught a couple of elderly ladies who were walking by the wall—but they didn't mind it; they just laughed, covered their heads, and scampered away.

The three of us sat around watching the wind play with the sea for an hour or two, but presently the wanderlust seduced us again and we (I) decided to walk along the seawall toward the south where there seemed to be a Coney Island affair with roller coasters and slides and brassy music all rearing its ugly head above the waters. This was Clarence Pier, the place where you can catch a Hovercraft to Gosport if you want one.

Hovercraft are the ultimate in amphibious travel: They can go anywhere on water and swampy areas because they ride on a pocket of air; the things can go at a breathtaking pace across the English Channel—from Dover to Oostende it takes them 30 minutes, whereas an old-fashioned ferry would take four hours. And the British Navy had a patent on it, although the British Rail system ran it. We watched the Hovercraft coming in furiously from Gosport and caroming to a halt in a cloud of dust on the beach at the pier. This was just a small version of the one they use for Channel crossings at Dover. Eventually British Rail wanted to start transatlantic Hovercraft service, but that never happened. The cross-channel service closed in 2000 because of the Channel Tunnel and larger and faster ferries and catamarans that could transport more automobiles across to the continent. Interest in Hovercraft waned and now they are primarily used for military amphibious operations, shallow-water search-and-rescue efforts, and sporting events.

The carnival area wasn't too interesting since it reminded us too much of America—not-so-cheap, plastic thrills. Something noteworthy happened, however, as we were strolling past the pier: a rowboat was capsized by a large wave and a man was floundering about half-naked in the icy water. He was having a hard time getting his boat right-side up, so another rowboatsman rowed up to him to help. The guy must have nearly frozen, because he was in the water for 20 minutes or so.

A little further along the coast we came across Southsea Castle, a fortress built in 1544 by Henry VIII to protect Portsmouth Harbour from the French and Spanish and other nasties. It certainly was an impregnable place. Jim, Steve, and I walked along the battlements, pretending to be loyal English soldiers of the Commonwealth searching the far horizon for the Dutch enemy fleet under Admirals Maarten Tromp and Michiel de Ruyter. But all we saw were a few distant merchant ships flying the Union Jack.

Jim and Steve weren't particularly interested in seeing the castle in great detail, but I dragged them through the sleeping quarters, the armory, and the supply room, which weren't really in too tremendous condition, but there they were, defending England along with the cannons. It did look rather imposing, from the outside at least. There was a miniature museum at the castle, and we paid the man a few pence to see it. They had interesting stuff there like relics from *HMS Bounty,* some flint arrowheads and pottery from the Wessex culture that inhabited southern England, and a few terracotta figurines that the Romans did not think important enough to take with them when they evacuated the island. Besides this, there were suits of armor worn by the defenders of the castle, eight or nine maps depicting the fortifications scattered around Portsmouth in the 1540s and how they were built, and a little gilded 15th-century Turkish cannon that was allegedly still in operating condition.

All this history was right up my alley, but Steve was beginning to weary of it, so we left the castle area and started back to the YMCA taking a circuitous route that brought us past a couple of large monuments to the Portsmouth-Southsea-Gosport veterans of World Wars I and II. Past these was Southsea Common, a large green playing field where some teenagers were playing some "football" (American soccer).

By this time, it was 7:00 p.m. and time for dinner at the Y. It was a fairly nourishing meal for 26p—a dirt-cheap price for the large amount of food we got. After dinner we took a quiet twilight stroll along the harbor until it got chilly around 9:00 p.m. Back at the YMCA, I watched a BBC program on the color telly. The program was a sort of comedy hour called *Up Pompeii* that was set in pre-eruption Italy. The MC was a famous British comedian named Frankie Howerd who oozed subtle double meanings from every pore. He and the rest of the guests were dressed up in Roman costumes to make things truly classical; their humor was British understatement aimed at politicians and social mores.

Then it was beddie-bye at 11:00 p.m.

Sunday, June 27, 1971

This morning I had a wild, ambitious plan to hitchhike up to Stonehenge to see a megalith or two. When I announced it to my fellow travelers, Steve was moderately enthused, but Jim complained of an upset stomach and said he didn't feel like going. I encouraged him to come along and told him that the best thing for butterflies in the tummy was a trip to Stonehenge. This only made him sicker, but he said he'd see how he felt after breakfast. Eggs and sausage didn't help his constitution any, and I suspect his illness was due to an overdose of nerves. Jim said thanks anyway, but he'd content himself by walking along the harbourfront and strolling down Commercial Road.

Steve and I asked the YMCA proprietor the best way to hitchhike to Salisbury. He said the best route to take was the road to Winchester (A33), although one would think the road though Southampton (A27) would have been better, since it's bigger and more direct. I believe he told us the way he would go if he were driving. But we didn't know anything about British roads then. The sky was all clouded up and we were worried about getting stuck in the rain, but the proprietor assured us that Merrie Olde England was usually clouded over and it wasn't really worth putting off a day's excursion for a few measly clouds. So off we went.

The first leg of our journey consisted of taking a green bus to Cosham again, since to begin hitchhiking, it's always best to get as far away from the center of town as possible. Cosham was the logical choice because we were already vaguely familiar with it and Winchester Road was only a few blocks away from the bus route. We kept pestering the bus driver to let us off at or near Winchester Road and he finally did, after a bit of grumbling, at 10:30 a.m.

Hitchhiking was still a common mode of transportation in both North America and Europe back in those days. When I was in high school in Columbus, Ohio, on many Saturdays I would hitchhike down High Street from the apartment where I lived with my father to visit the library at Ohio State University. One of the first summer jobs I ever had was as a caddy at the OSU golf course, something my father insisted I do so that I would "appreciate the value of money." However, he could not always give me a ride there, so many times I wound up hitchhiking. Luckily, I never had any problems except for occasional delays and, as you will see, the system often worked well enough if you placed yourself in the right spot, were patient, and had a backup plan if things got too frustrating.

We still had to walk a bit before we got to the highway, but we tried hitching anyway. Nothing happened. We saw two girls hitching on the other side of the street and they managed to find a ride all right. Their technique was a bit different from ours: They were walking along with the traffic trailing their thumbs behind them and shaking them in the direction they were walking. Steve and I figured this was the way it was done in England, so we practiced their technique and perfected it, but we still didn't get a ride.

We almost missed the Winchester turnoff because the British road signs are damned confusing and the road was smaller than we thought it would be. Finally, a friendly young Britisher picked us up and gave us a short ride up the hill. He was headed for an even smaller road in the direction of Southwick, I believe, and the Forest of Bere. He let us off at the turnoff where an ice cream stand was located. We stood there by the side of the road overlooking the hill of Ports Down on our right. The view was very nice—all sorts of little fields scattered over the plain and dotted with bushes, stray rocks, and cows in the foreground.

We tried all sorts of thumbing tricks, but none of them worked. One or two people stopped, but they said that they were going in a different direction from the one we wanted. Looking back on it all now, I think we were somehow on the wrong road. Anyway, about 12:30 p.m. we became discouraged and felt that if we were going to get anywhere at all today, we would have to spend a few shillings. So we trekked the long way back to Cosham (and had no luck hitchhiking in this direction either), found the Cosham bus station, and bought tickets to Salisbury, which is the largest town near Stonehenge. We figured we'd have plenty of time to thumb the 10 miles or so to Amesbury and Stonehenge.

We were glad we had stopped thumbing because it started to drizzle a bit. We got to Salisbury in practically no time at all, walked from the station through town past a 14th-century monument-like structure near the center of town called the Poultry Cross, and found the road to Amesbury, which was only about 9 miles away. This time we were luckier and found a good ride all the way to Stonehenge. Our chauffeur was a friendly thirtyish man who was interested in the way Americans drive cars. He said he had seen a program on the BBC that featured a few ghastly accidents on some of our Interstates, and he thought perhaps the problem might be that Americans have such big cars that it's really hard to miss smashing into each other when you're driving. By some strange quirk of Fate, Steve had seen the same show either on American TV or as a movie feature some months earlier. The two of them discussed the relative merits of American and British drivers.

We passed a place called Boscombe Down and the driver explained that this was where the Royal Air Force is testing experimental aircraft and missiles. He said the neighbors were a bit vexed that all this was going on but, after all, it's all for the glory of Britannia and you never know when a war might flare up in your own back yard, ha ha. Boscombe Down is not the only place in the area where the RAF and the Army have testing grounds; stations like this are dotted all around the fields and woods of Salisbury Plain. During the war, Stonehenge was used to test the feasibility of flash photography from a moving aircraft to behind-the-lines reconnaissance. Wiltshire has always been a popular military spot because it is such a wide-open area.

At last, we got out of the car and approached the stony Druid giants. They faced outwards, ready to meet attack from all directions. Grim remnants of that sacred druidic era of oak, golden sickles, and mistletoe, they shrieked a stern, silent warning to the bold American invaders. Yet the giants moved not. I immediately went into Celtic mythological mode, imagining them as Caugherigan and Tregeagle from Dozmary Pool, the home of the Lady of the Lake; Little Grim from Lincoln; Bolster, the Cornish giant of Portreath; Trecobben of the ten fingers; Termagol with his trident arms; Palug the mighty cat whose jaws of fire melt all bronze; the tusk-toothed Chief of Annwfn, the Welsh Otherworld; Tyrnoc with his head of vipers and Pen Palach of the oaken skull; Manawydan, Welsh hero of the dark net; and Pryderi, the king of Dyfed, who leaves no shadow, so black is he—all were present. The Celts were not a people to do things in a small way. Only megalithic giants could serve as their altar.

Steve and I explored Stonehenge more closely. In 1971, visitors to Stonehenge were allowed to wander through the site and touch the stones; since 1977, the site has been roped off and visitors can only walk around the circle from a short distance away. We noted there were two basic types of stones. The bigger vertical stones were the sarsens, a kind of natural sandstone that forms huge boulders on the surface of the Marlborough Downs 20 miles away—these were set up around 2500 BCE by the Bell Beaker people from the eastern Mediterranean; the way these stones were squared and dressed indicated to us that they were influenced by Minoan Crete, since no one else back then was really into grandiose megalithic architecture.

The Sarsen Circle was set up to replace the much older Bluestone Circle of about 60 chunks of blue-colored rock that had been hauled by some Neolithic culture from the Preseli Hills in southwestern Wales. The bluestones weren't just thrown away, however, when the sarsens replaced them—later on they were set up within the Sarsen Circle to make it look prettier. The whole thing was finished about 1600 BCE, long before the Celtic Druids ever lived in England. It is now known that Stonehenge dates much further back, all the way to 3000 BCE as a circular bank-and-ditch enclosure. But the Druids still hold their midsummer ceremonies there and, as a matter of fact, if we had gotten there a few days earlier we could have observed it all. Of course, there are no real Druids left, only some pretend ones, but it's all formal and esoteric and very Celtic.

There were a couple other odd stones: A flat one called the Altar Stone, which was formerly supposed to have been where the Druids sacrificed things; and a triangular upright one called the Heel Stone, which, when you frame it between two stones in the Sarsen Circle at sunrise on midsummer's day, the sun will creep up over its top. Amazing structure, really. Using a similar method, you can also look at the midwinter moonrise. The ancients knew what they were doing.

Steve and I lazed around for 25 minutes picking up all sorts of megalithic vibes. There were a couple freaky stoner types (how appropriate) sitting out on the mound past the Aubrey Holes who apparently were tuned in to some primeval mystical wavelength. After a while I went and took some photos of the rocks and Steve took a photo of me being sacrificed on the Altar Stone, but it never came out well because my camera shutter was acting up. They were all double-exposed.

I forgot to mention it before, but you have to pay to go see Britain's oldest tourist attraction. They've charged 10p for the past year or so! Prior to that it was free. Needless to say, red-blooded Englishmen were up in arms about it—they felt the place is too sacred (like their cathedrals) to charge money to see it.

After a bit, we decided to leave and try to get back to Salisbury in time to see Old Sarum, which is on a hill outside of town. Actually, it is nothing more than the site of the medieval town of Salisbury, but it was supposed to be interesting.

After hitchhiking a few minutes the European way, we got a ride with three girls and a guy, all students, who had just been to Stonehenge. Their small car was packed with all six of us in it, but they were only going two miles away to Amesbury, so we clambered in and clambered out.

By this time, it was about 3:00 p.m. and Steve's digestive juices were beginning to flow, so we looked for a place to eat. But this was Sunday, the day when everything in Britain but Scotland Yard closes down. Sundays are very bleak days for travelers— there is absolutely nothing to do except, of course, visit places like Stonehenge. The only place open in Amesbury was a fast-food cafeteria with cheap-tasting, expensive food. Steve satiated his appetite temporarily with something or other, while I wasted my shillings on a salad.

We now had to hitchhike back to Salisbury and, based on our good luck in coming from there, we thought we stood a decent chance of going back. Such was not the case. We walked and walked and walked and thumbed, but what little traffic there was didn't see fit to give us a lift, although we were thumbing according to European rules.

I was kind of eager for a nice hike through the English countryside though and didn't particularly mind our bad luck. The day had started out drizzly, but by the time afternoon rolled around it was rather pleasant and sunny. It was a long, long way to Salisbury and before too long our feet were beginning to complain. Steve had never done much hiking before (his mother said it was too dangerous), but I felt he had potential, and when his strength began to wane, I urged him on to greater efforts and told him Salisbury was just over the next ridge. After a dozen ridges, Steve began to feel that I had no sense of distance, but I told him, no, I knew exactly where I was and if he felt that I was not an adequate leader, well then he could just find a saber and heroically point the way home himself. All this raillery gave us further energy to make the hike.

Another source of energy were some porno magazines and pictorial "how-to" books we found in a ditch by the road. We read these as we marched along. Very edifying, it was. Somewhere along the way, we stopped at a petrol station to see if they had a water fountain, but we discovered (to our dismay) that, in Britain at least, drinking fountains were rare, especially in petrol stations.

Finally, after walking no less than six miles, a middle-aged lady driver felt sorry for us and stopped. She gave us a ride the rest of the way into Salisbury, an act of kindness for which we have been forever thankful. Our plans to see Old Sarum had to be scrapped because we needed to get back to Portsmouth before nightfall. No doubt Jim was having conniptions about us already.

A train ride from Salisbury got us back to Cosham around 8:00 p.m. There we caught a red bus and arrived at Clarence Pier at 8:30. We scurried back up to the YMCA where we found Jim, remarkably unflustered for the amount of worry we must have caused him. He said he felt a lot better and had a splendid time walking around the harbourfront and the downtown area, pondering the mysteries of existence.

Since by this time it was 9:00, dinner at the YMCA had been long over, but their snack bar was still open and the man cooked us up some meat pies (sort of like pot pies, but not really) and shook us up some milk (not a milkshake, but literally "shaken milk") and we had to be content with this. Since it was Sunday, there wasn't much else open this late. After our snack, we waited around and read newspapers and watched people play foosball until the proprietor came around; we had to pay him for another night's stay.

Tomorrow our adventure would really begin: We must journey to the Isle of Wight to see whether we had jobs and whether Steve's stamped passport would prevent him from getting employment—we also had to see if the Anglo-America Association was the kind of organization worthy of our love and reverence.

Monday, June 28, 1971

At 8:00 we greeted the dawn and ate our free cafeteria breakfast downstairs. Afterward, I gathered up my change and put in a call to the Anglo-America Association and explained our situation to Mrs. Richardson. Since Steve had his passport stamped by the customs authorities, she said, there was no way they could legally get him a job. Restrictions on foreign work permits were stiff due to there being so many people already in England who needed jobs. But there was work waiting for Jim and me, details to be given when we arrived on the Isle of Wight. We told Mrs. Richardson we were on our merry way out the door, then we bid farewell to the YMCA keeper and hustled on down to the Isle of Wight ferry down in the dockyard. We were still a bit early, so we hung around outside the Lloyd's of London bank across the street until it opened. We got our traveler's checks converted, then rushed over to the ferry where we bought a fairly inexpensive ticket to Ryde, as it were, on the Isle of Wight.

We secured a spot near the bow of the ferry where we could see all the action. When the boat was ready to push off, one of the younger hands (a slender lad of 14) was having trouble pulling in the mooring rope, or whatever sailors call it. He wasn't using the capstan correctly, so the skipper came over to help him. This skipper was a fantastic specimen of humanity. He wore a traditional blue sailor's cap that hung cockily on the back of his skull like a jib sail. This was balanced by a splendid Lord Kitchener mustache that cascaded magnificently from his upper lip like the Horseshoe Falls at Niagara. He also wore a blue pea jacket that he never buttoned up, exposing his luxuriantly hairy chest to the lash of salt spray that whipped in from the ocean. He was the epitome of Salty Dogness. Anyway, the skipper showed this youngster how to pull the rope in correctly, but the lad kept on botching it, so with two dozen salty curses the skipper pushed his hand out of the way, dramatically seized the capstan and the rope, and hauled the rope in himself, all the time shouting, "This 'ere's 'ow ye do 'er, mate!"

The voyage didn't take too long, 45 minutes at most, and we amused ourselves by watching the skipper pose heroically in the bow of his ship. Somehow we never thought to take a photo of the chap—if we had, I know it would have made a good *Life* magazine cover.

As soon as we landed at Ryde, we found a bus and took it to Newport, the largest city on the island and headquarters of the Anglo-America Association. The bus was fairly exquisite, at least compared to the ones we had experienced in Portsmouth. The ride from Ryde was scenic. We went up and down all sorts of forested rills and valleys with little villages perched on and planted in them. You see, the Isle of Wight is mostly inhabited by retired colonels and such who have purchased a villa on the island because the climate is so mild in comparison to the rest of the ruddy country. The beaches and resorts here are popular in the summer too, and this attracts people with money.

In Newport we asked a few people where Pyle Street was and found it wasn't too far from the bus station. So we found the Anglo-America place at 60A Pyle Street and walked upstairs and into the door where we were greeted by a couple of young and winsome secretaries. Mrs. Richardson was there too, in her own office next to that of Neil Ray's, the director.

Mrs. R. was a friendly, reddish-haired, secretary-looking type of about 32 who sat us down right away and discussed our problems. First off, she repeated how impossible it was for Steve to get a job—there was a slim chance that he could have it reversed, but it would take five months. We had hoped that if Steve left the country and went to, say, Holland, then came back and talked to the customs man again, that he could get fixed up that way. That wouldn't work, she said.

Second, Mrs. R. explained that because of the incredible UK postal workers strike from January 20 through March 8, 1971, Anglo-America's usual employers hadn't been able to mail their job notices out to the association at all. They were forced to fill the vacancies on their own. Thus jobs were pretty scarce even if your passport wasn't stamped as restricted.

Third, Mrs. R. assured us that there were still jobs available for us on the Isle of Wight—all she had to do was call up an agency or two and we were hired. That sounded good to Jim, who just wanted any old sort of job, but I had been hoping for hospital work. Mrs. R. said that hospitals didn't like to hire temporary help even if it was experienced help, but she was nice enough to call up a hospital or two to confirm her doubts.

Fourth, she called a couple numbers and got Jim a job at Warner's Chalet Hotel near Yarmouth, about 10 miles away. The official title was "dining room assistant," and she said there was another opening for me if I wanted it. I said I didn't really know, and could I think about it for an hour or so, then come back? Mrs.

R. said that was just fine since she was about to leave for lunch, and she told us to come back anytime after a half hour.

Jim, Steve, and I walked back outside and found a place where we bought a loaf of bread and some fruit, which we gobbled down eagerly in a small park with "keep off the grass" signs on it. Jim was feeling responsible now. He had a job and his brother didn't, so he felt that he had to somehow provide him with a place to stay and some grocery money. Steve felt a bit guilty about that and he thought he could just send home for some money to tide him over until his return flight. This return flight was not particularly a problem, since Mrs. Richardson had said she would reserve seats for us on almost any date we wished. But Steve was jobless and this might necessitate returning a bit earlier.

After our refreshing outdoor lunch, we strolled back to Pyle Street and Mrs. R. to take care of the rest of our business. To make a long story short, Jim confirmed his job, I decided not to take a job (at least through the Anglo-America Association), Jim and Steve would return September 1 or thereabouts, and I would return on September 9—all we had to do was contact the Seaglair travel agency in London sometime this summer to pick up our tickets. Seaglair was the Canadian outfit that had done all the work of getting us a flight out of the US. Mrs. R. was also nice enough to refund the $25 I had paid Anglo-America to get me a job— unfortunately, it was an Ohio National Bank check, since Neil Ray, the director of Anglo-America, had an account there. This seemed a bit strange, but I didn't worry about it at the time.

We said goodbye to Mrs. Richardson, having in general received a favorable impression of Anglo-America. However, we hoped we wouldn't have to be doing business with them in the future, since that would probably mean trouble.

Our next stop was Yarmouth, a sleepy little fishing village on the west coast of the Isle of Wight, which we attained after an uneventful bus ride. Just a short walk from the bus station took us to Warner's Chalet Hotel, where Jim would be working for the next month or so. This was a moderately luxurious place, now known as Warner Hotels, Norton Grange, with pleasant little gardens and walks and a swimming pool and cottage-type quarters and a mansion-type lodge. We stuck our heads in the dining room and saw quite a few teenagers bustling around with trays and menus, setting tables for lunch. The whole joint just reeked of placid aristocracy, and to make things totally outrageous, it wasn't meant as a resort for placid aristocrats—it was meant as a summer camp of sorts for their equally placid children.

The three of us walked into the reception area of the lodge and asked for the manager, Mr. Robertson. This chap was a tall, clean-cut young fellow who greeted us warmly and got Jim to feeling at home right away. We told Mr. Robertson about Steve's passport problem and asked if perhaps there would be room for Steve to bunk with his brother here for a while until some money came in from the US. Unfortunately, he said this wouldn't work because the place was overcrowded as it was. He explained to Jim where his sleeping quarters were, then told him to get freshened up and get back by 4:00 p.m. to start serving dinner, hinting that the other two of us should get lost by then.

We hiked over to Jim's new bunk area, which was a one-room cottage with two beds and a sink and a toilet. We thought it was strange that Mr. Robertson had said there was no room for Steve, yet there was an extra bunk that no one was using. Anyway, we felt it would be too risky for Jim's job if we tried to smuggle Steve in here for a few days, and I knew Jim would feel no end of guilt about it, so we decided against it. However, something had to be done with Steve since he was so helpless by himself.

I was anxious to leave for the continent because my friend Dave Hall in the US Army in Germany was getting ready any day now to go on a 15-day leave, and I wanted to be there when that happened. So I proposed to Steve that he tag along to Europe with me and provide me with laughter and companionship for a while until he could look up a German relative or two that he said he had hidden away in the Rhineland. Steve thought this was a splendid idea, but Jim naturally had reservations, so I assured him that I'd make Steve write him and his mother every other day, especially if we were dying of pneumonia or stuck in jail. I reckoned we might as well take our time and do things leisurely, since we had some two months before our return.

The Isle of Wight was a rather pleasant destination on its own and we could explore it a bit, I figured. Steve dropped off his suitcase and I dropped my sleeping bag and backpack off at Jim's quarters, having decided to trek down to Yarmouth to buy a sleeping bag and backpack for Steve, who was ill-equipped for foraging in the wilderness with a cumbersome suitcase. We'd sleep in the boondocks under a starry British sky tonight, then leave tomorrow or the next day for Deutschland.

Gear was expensive in Yarmouth, but the store owner recommended a place in Freshwater, a village a couple of miles inland. Since evening was approaching, we decided to hitchhike, and before long we were picked up by a friendly middle-aged lady who took us straight to the front door of the store we wanted. This store had everything we needed—low-priced sleeping bags and backpacks. Steve bought one of each (all for £3.40) and was going to buy a canteen if they had one, but it seems canteens are a peculiarly American commodity and the closest thing they had was a bulky, plastic, quart-size container.

Next door at a market we bought a loaf of bread and some milk. We saved the bread for later and drank the milk. After this, we hitchhiked back to Yarmouth, getting a ride almost immediately. Our whole trip only took an hour! Rather encouraging compared to the delays we experienced around Stonehenge.

Back at Warner's Chalet Hotel, Jim was still learning how to wait on tables, so I had to sneak into the kitchen to ask him to give me the key to his cottage so we could re-pack Steve's luggage and maybe brush our teeth. Jim was pretty muddled from waiting on so many tables. I didn't blame him this time—his supervisor was a young and very strict blonde who knew how to give orders; she almost threw me out. It took him about 15 minutes to get around to giving me the key. All he had to do was reach into his pocket, but somehow that was complicated. We got Steve's necessaries stuffed in his new backpack, stopped off at the dining room to tell Jim we'd see him tomorrow, and walked back into Yarmouth to find a post office.

We bought some stamps for our letters home. I also attempted to contact someone in the US Army who would know where Dave Hall, my Army friend, was stationed—perhaps I could even leave a message for him or talk to him personally. I was trying to phone a German operator who seemed to be on the right track, but we kept getting cut off. German phone systems are even worse than British ones, and when you combine the two, the result is impossible. After a while I gave up.

Steve and I found a public footpath to Freshwater and set out upon it. Public footpaths are a universal European phenomenon—in Germany they are called Wanderwege, in Wales they are Llwybrau cerdded (however you pronounce that). But they all serve the same function of giving the average city- or village-dweller some place to go when he wants to escape to the greenery. There are countless numbers of them scattered around the countryside.

We walked up the Freshwater footpath until we found a nice woodsy spot to relieve ourselves and conceal our gear, then returned for a 1½-mile gearless hike into town. The sun was setting, the crows (or ravens) were squawking, and the evening breezes were beginning to blow in from the sea. It was all so pastoral. We ate up that loaf of bread we'd bought earlier and discussed literature. I was surprised to discover that Steve had read Theodore Roszak's *The Making of a Counter-Culture* (1969), a relatively difficult book that no one else I know (other than Dave Hall) has read. You just never know about people.

When we got to Freshwater we found a cozy little pub called the Royal Standard Hotel and had a couple of beers apiece. Steve's Black Labels only cost him 10p this time. Having those glasses of stout made the walk back seem a lot better. By this time, it was 9:00 p.m. or so and the stars were coming out. It was a beautiful night. The English countryside after dark is peaceful and timeless. Half close your eyes and you can see the 15th century passing in front of you. We got back to our gear without incident, except near Freshwater we ran into a couple of hunters out "potting" for pigeon. They hallooed us and we hallooed back. Friendly hunters, those. We found a nice comfy spot in an open field and spread out our sleeping bags. This was Steve's first night out camping ever, but he seemed like he was willing to have a go at being rugged. We dozed off watching the twinklings of a thousand heavenly lamps burning in the ebon firmament.

Thus ends the narrative that I had expanded from my trip diary after I returned home. College courses just got in the way. This explains why the daily entries for the remainder of this European adventure are less detailed.

Tuesday, June 29, 1971

Steve and I woke up at 5:30 a.m. to a cloudy sky and dew adorning the grass. It was drizzling a bit. We walked back to Yarmouth and hung around the pier until some of the businesses opened up. Some swans were swimming about in the cold. We dozed, wrote letters, and talked.

At 8:00 a.m., we went to a place called The Gallery for coffee and eats. This establishment featured a large geological map of the Isle of Wight on the wall. It indicated there were many fossils to be found on the coast around Freshwater Bay, so we decided we might hike over there and look for ammonites and petrified wood.

But first we wandered back to Warner's Chalet Hotel and got the key from Jim so that we could stow our stuff temporarily in his cottage room. The kitchen there was a madhouse. We gave Jim back his key and walked back through Yarmouth to start hitchhiking to Newport.

After 30 minutes we got a ride all the way to town with a couple of retired rich types in their 50s who were very friendly. In Newport, we went to the Anglo-America Association office to straighten out the business of Steve's revised airplane ticket. I also tried to call Dave in Germany, with no luck. The Army didn't seem to know he existed.

We bought some bread and fruit in one of the markets, then had some lunch after walking the wrong way out of Newport. After a while we got a ride from a Scotsman who told us all about Scotland and how much better it was there. He was very friendly though.

Steve and I walked back about two miles into Freshwater and quickly got lost along the wrong road. Then we discovered a fort-like structure called the Freshwater Redoubt, built in 1856, and a public footpath through a jungle of weird, wind-blasted trees. We walked along this path, which must have been the Tennyson Trail, south to Freshwater Bay on the south coast. It was a beautiful sight, reminiscent of Thomas Hardy's *Far from the Madding Crowd.* We saw many seagulls and, high on a chalk down, we ran across a tall cross-shaped memorial, the Alfred, Lord Tennyson Monument. The Victorian poet had lived nearby with his wife Emily in a house on Freshwater Bay for 39 years, until his death in 1892. "The Charge of the Light Brigade" and many more of his poems were inspired by the magnificent rocky headlands and misty sunrises that Tennyson encountered as he walked along the down.

Energized by the spirit of Tennyson, I told Steve, "Half a league, half a league, half a league onward for some geological fun!" Though exhausted, we walked along the top of the sea cliff, then stumbled down to the shoreline and did some beachcombing, finding some polished rocks and a few fossils. The ocean waves were hypnotic.

We tried to hitchhike back to Yarmouth, with no success at all. So we walked back to Freshwater to go to the Royal Standard Hotel again. Steve and I discussed the lack of canteens and the issue of warm British beer with the pub's bartender as we ordered a Bloody Mary and two cold beers. While there, we met another long-haired American from Colorado with whom we compared our experiences in England. He was apparently having mixed thumbing results too.

Another hitchhiking attempt to Yarmouth met with no success, so we wound up walking 2½ more miles to Warner's Chalet Hotel and met up with Jim. We washed up in Jim's room and adjusted Steve's luggage. Then we bade farewell to Jim, wishing him all the best with his summer of labor.

We ran into the night security guard at the hotel. He was an interesting vagabond who said he had spent some time in a Canadian jail. He gave us a tip on where to sleep. There was an abandoned barn outside of Freshwater near the Brambles Chine Holiday Camp, a little way to the southwest. He said he had slept there the previous week. We found the Brambles and bedded down in the barn around 9:30–10:00 p.m. The hay had a fantastic smell and was very comfy.

Wednesday, June 30, 1971

Steve and I awoke at 8:00 a.m. to the sound of some kind of animal scrambling on the roof of the barn. We partook of some bread before making the long walk to the outskirts of Freshwater, where we hoped to catch a ride back to Newport.

We had a long wait at an intersection with no hitchhiking luck, so we walked down the road to a turnoff and had more success there. A businessman picked us up and let us off outside Newport. He was friendly and told us all about the Isle of Wight Rock Festival at Afton Down on August 26–31, 1970. The lineup was spectacular, with Jimi Hendrix, Chicago, The Doors, The Moody Blues, Procol Harum, The Who, Miles Davis, Joan Baez, Joni Mitchell, Jethro Tull, Donovan, Sly and the Family Stone, Ten Years After, Emerson Lake & Palmer, Tiny Tim, and Free. When I got back to Columbus, I bought the live album of Hendrix playing at the festival—it's one of his best. Apparently, the event was larger than Woodstock, with some 600,000–700,000 people attending. The businessman said the only difficulty the organizers had was with "some French and Algerians," probably referring to some anarchists who had threatened people with knives on the ferry crossing.

We walked through Newport and called the Anglo-America Association to verify Steve's return flight. Everything was in order, so we located the road to Ryde and after a short wait got a ride from a Liverpool couple who took us directly to the pier. We got on the ferry almost immediately, but not the one with the colorful skipper that we observed on the way over. The ferry arrived back in Portsmouth around 11:30 a.m.

Our destination was Germany, but first we had to travel to Dover to take a ferry across the English Channel. We found a Wimpy restaurant and had burgers for lunch for 30p. Then we took the by-now-familiar red bus to Cosham.

We began hitchhiking east at the edge of Cosham and were soon picked up by a guy who was originally from India but who had lived all over the place. Now he worked at IBM as an electronic engineer. He enjoyed our youthful freedom and said he was tied down in the British rat race. "That is so much better than the American rat race," I reassured him. He told us there are some Americans who have chosen to live in England because it is so much slower here. He let us off after about five miles at Havant, in Hampshire to the northeast of Portsmouth.

Then we were picked up by a couple who were planning to visit South Africa soon. They took us about 30 miles and let us off outside of Worthing in West Sussex. Soon afterward we got a ride from a student who was going to Brighton, about 12 miles away. He let us off near the Royal Pavilion, the seaside retreat of the Prince of Wales who later became King George IV in 1820–1830. We took a short tour of this amazing edifice, which was built in 1787 in an Indian architectural style, complete with many onion domes and minarets and a lavish neoclassical interior.

We then poked around the student sector of the University of Sussex in nearby Kemptown. After that we took a bus to what we thought was the A27 road to Lewes. But the driver had steered us wrong, putting us instead on the A23 road to London. Annoyed, we found we were a full three miles away from our intended hitchhiking road. Luckily, we got a ride to the A27 from a student driving a small car.

After a short time, we were picked up by a fisherman who took us all the way, some 18 miles, to Eastbourne in a gray, square-back, truck-like vehicle. Outside Eastbourne, we got a short ride from a guy in a Jaguar going 90 mph.

Finally, we had some true success with a red-haired guy nicknamed Ginge (for Ginger; actual name, William Ian McNeill) who took us the entire 65 miles to Dover because, like us, he was headed for the English Channel ferry to the Continent. Ginge was in the army but was on leave so he could visit a friend and his wife for a week. He was born in Scotland, but had been all over Germany, North Africa, Singapore, and England. He had been a hippie in London in the Flower Power year of 1965, sitting around for hours holding his friends' hands, meditating, and drinking

41

green mint tea, or so he claimed. He was a horny character and shared some salacious stories with us about his escapades.

Ginge took local roads so that he could drive by the ruins of Hastings Castle and, later on, Dover Castle to show us what they looked like. He let us off to wander around while he got his car safely on board, saying he would see us on the ferry later. Meanwhile, Steve and I gawked at the famed White Cliffs of Dover—they appeared a bit grayer than I expected, probably due to the streaks of black flint that dampened the bright white of the chalk.

Steve and I did a student thing and attempted to get on the English Channel ferry for free, but our ruse failed, and we had to pay £2 each for tickets. We had a long wait, so we decided to eat dinner at a restaurant in the terminal. At last, we boarded the ferry and located Ginge, who treated us to cider and beer. We climbed the stairs to an upper deck where we found seats with a view and discussed music and chicks and many other things. Ginge soon got a bit seasick, so he decided to sack out for a while. Steve and I dozed off and on as the ferry progressed. I do not remember with any certainty, but I think the ship was operated by Townsend Thoresen Ferries.

Thursday, July 1, 1971

Our ferry arrived in Zeebrugge, Belgium, late—around 4:30 a.m. or so. We had gotten very little sleep, and it took the longest time for Ginge to get off the ferry with his car. He was headed somewhere else, perhaps to the Netherlands, but he said he would give us a ride into Germany, as our first destination was Köln (Cologne). We went through customs, then slept most of the way in the car as Ginge drove through Belgium and Holland. It was flat, uninteresting country anyway. Saw only one windmill. I woke up briefly to see the many large, bourgeois houses in Antwerp.

Ginge drove us into Kaldenkirchen, Germany, on the Dutch border along the Meuse River. Steve and I gave him tremendous thanks for the ride and wished him a happy visit with his friends.

We walked into town, the awareness suddenly hitting us for the first time that we were in a non-English-speaking country.

Our first priority was finding a bank. In those days, credit cards were just getting started up (I certainly did not have one) and ATMs were rare and bank-specific, so to cash traveler's checks or obtain coins and paper money we had to use various financial services provided by local banks, currency exchanges, or (preferably) American Express offices that offered Americans a better rate. I was not very good at speaking German, but we managed to get some traveler's checks cashed.

We went to a bakery and bought bread and some pastries, then went to the train station and bought a ticket to Köln. It was a bit confusing at the small Bahnhof—we had to ask people which train was the one to Köln, where Köln was, and so on. The city would be hard to miss, for it is on the west bank of the Rhine River and the fourth most populous in Germany.

After we arrived at the Hauptbahnhof in Köln, about a two-hour ride, we wandered around helplessly until I bought a city map and located a nearby Jugendherberge (youth hostel), probably what is now the A&O Hostel Köln Dom. We hoofed it to the hostel around 11:50 a.m. and waited until it opened 30 minutes later and went in, paid, and checked our luggage.

Steve and I had to wait until 5:00 p.m. when our rooms would be ready, so to pass the time we went to the Cologne Zoological Garden, the third oldest zoo in Germany. We saw all sorts of fearsome beasts—penguins and bears and birds and primates and elephants and antelopes and an aquarium and an insectarium. We hiked back to the hostel and got there in time for dinner at 6:00 p.m. It was a terrible dinner that cost us DM 1.20 for a lousy serving. After dinner I went right to bed and slept for 12 hours while Steve rapped with some guy from New Jersey who said how terrible things were in Berlin.

Friday, July 2, 1971

At 7:00 a.m. I woke up to Bob Dylan music playing over the loudspeaker, the signal that breakfast was about to be served.

Steve and I decided not to eat at the hostel, so we walked down to the city's medieval cathedral, the Kölner Dom, around 10:00 a.m. and paid 50pf to walk up the 489 steps (as I wrote at the time)—or was it the 533 steps that the guidebooks say now?—to the observation platform in the south spire. About 515 feet in height, the cathedral is the tallest twin-spired church in the world and is visited by huge numbers of tourists every year. Construction began in 1248, but the church was not completed until 1880, for many different reasons. It was about a 15-minute climb up the stairs that go past the belfry housing one of the huge cathedral bells, the Petersglocke (the locals have nicknamed it "Fat Peter"). From the observation platform, we were treated to a grand view of the city and the Rhine River.

At the cathedral, we met three travelers: a guy from New Jersey, a Scottish fellow, and Geoff Reed from Lafayette, Louisiana. It was a friendly group, so we decided to visit a bierkeller and sample the local brews. Outside, we ran into another American, Judy from California, who had just arrived from the airport, and invited her to come along with us. At the bierkeller, I had a Kölsch, a pale, light-bodied beer brewed in Köln, and we all talked for a long time.

The New Jersey and Scotland guys had to leave to catch a plane, so Geoff and Judy and Steve and I decided we would attempt to purchase tickets for a riverboat cruise down the Rhine. A nice introduction to the delights of Deutschland!

First, we bought some food for lunch. Geoff stashed his luggage in a locker, then we went to a museum down the road—probably the Wallraf-Richartz Museum—and saw all sorts of Roman and medieval artifacts. One museum guide was very friendly, about 62 years old, and spoke some German to Judy, which she didn't understand.

We went into an Indian store for about 1½ hours and talked to Sid the proprietor. Geoff really wanted to buy a fancy chess set that the store had on display. Sid tried very hard to sell something to Judy but he failed. He finally gave her an ivory bookmark and he gave Steve a hand-woven napkin ring.

The four of us went back to the hostel after Geoff picked up his luggage from the train station locker. We bought a delicious apple pie in a bakery, split it four ways, and ate it in a park near the hostel. We tried to photograph some little German kids playing with matches, but they ran away.

Back at the hostel, Judy went right to bed because she was jet-lagged and exhausted from her recent plane trip. Later on, Geoff and Steve and I went out for some beer and had some warm Frikadelle (minced-meat patties) and discussed the ultimate meaninglessness of life. We crept back in good spirits to the hostel where our hostelmates were all asleep.

Saturday, July 3, 1971

I arose at 7:00 a.m., breakfast time. I located Judy and consoled her because her backpack had been either broken into or stolen. Geoff, Steve, and I said goodbye and wished her well on her further adventures.

The three of us tried to go to the bank, but it was closed on Saturday. Geoff went back to Sid's Indian store to haggle about the chess set, but he ultimately decided not to buy it, because he'd either have to lug it around or pay big bucks to ship it back to Louisiana.

Next we had to go to the train station to get some cash. We waited in line for a while but got a good exchange rate. At 10:00 a.m., we bought tickets for the Wiesbaden Rheinschifffahrt and boarded the riverboat for a cruise down the Rhine. The captain told us he was only going to Andernach, but we could catch another riverboat there to go further upriver.

On board were groups of happy Germans singing "Wunderbar," "Der Schöne, Schöne Rhein," and a Deutsche version of "Sloop John B" by the Beach Boys. The scenery was mostly industrial until we got past Bonn, then it became hilly and more rural. We passed our first castles—Drachenfels and Rolandsbogen. We met some high school girls—two from Brussels, one from Miami, and one from Peoria, Illinois—and blabbed a bit.

We drank a lot of beer and ate a bit of bread that we had bought in Köln. I took many photos of the Rhine scenery. Steve

45

was still obsessing about the lack of ice water and chilled beer. An oom-pah band was playing German music as new people boarded the boat in Königswinter.

Around 4:00 p.m., we arrived at the end of the line, Andernach, a scenic little town founded by the Romans way back in 12 BCE, and we bought tickets for another riverboat to continue our journey the following day. I had a fish sandwich (Filiert) and french fries (Pommes frites), then bought some film for my camera.

The three of us decided to look for a place to camp out. We stowed our luggage beneath an Autobahn overpass (probably the Krahnenbergbrücke) in a rugged area on a hill. We walked a short way toward another town in the forest along a Wanderweg (public footpath). The forest scenery was delightful, so we decided to sleep along this path later. Back in town, we ate more fish filets and went to a pub for some beer and got our canteen filled. The town had a red-light district (with a couple of genuinely red lights), where we happened to observe a *fille de joie* plying her trade.

Geoff, Steve, and I returned to where we stashed our luggage and brought it to our sleeping spot. However, we left our only canteen at the stash, and I had to go back for it. It was quite dark by the time we got all settled down. We ate some bananas and tomatoes and other food we had purchased in Andernach, then crawled into our sleeping bags. Geoff, who was from Louisiana, was a bit cold. We saw some fireworks going off in the distance, perhaps launched by some expatriate Americans for the Fourth of July.

Sunday, July 4, 1971

We woke up around 5:00 a.m. and had beans for breakfast, which we cooked on Geoff's butane stove. A few people started walking on the Wanderweg about 7:30 or 8:00. We went on a longish hike along the river and pretended we could see, off in the foggy distance, Siegfried slaying the dragon Fáfnir who was guarding the Nibelungen treasure horde. There were scenic overlooks, benches, and guys jogging. We scrambled up on slippery leaves to a plateau on top of a high hill where there were cycle and car tire marks. Many bugs beset us.

Then it was time to go back into town to buy wine and food for the continuation of our long boat ride on the Rhine. We bought three bottles of Apfelwein at the last minute because the store closed for lunch from 11:00–11:30. Our boat arrived at 11:30. It was crowded.

I was smitten watching a beautiful young Mädchen on the lower deck. She eventually came up to our deck and asked us for cigarettes. Geoff provided some. Her name was Angela and we talked to her for three hours as we passed legendary castles along the shore. Geoff was smitten too. Angela was 16 years old and liked American music. She was with her parents who were on board. We drank some wine and then she disembarked at Boppard around 2:00 p.m.

Then we talked to another girl who was with a tour group, but she got off at Sankt Goarshausen. We passed by many more scenic cliffs and fantastic castles, including the 13th-century Burg Rheinfels. We cruised by the famed Lorelei cliff, home of the enchanting siren who sat on top and combed her golden hair, distracting boatmen with her beauty and song and causing them to crash on the rocks.

We saw all sorts of barges and houseboats and cruise boats. We tried to cook the tinned sausage we had purchased in Andernach, but it had spoiled and we had to throw it overboard. But we were content with our bottles of Apfelwein and some tomatoes and other small fare.

All three of us began to get weary of the long boat ride, so on the spur of the moment we got off at Aßmannshausen at 7:45 p.m. to try to find a place to stay. The village is known for its red wine made from Pinot Noir grapes, and I'd already heard about it from a song on my *German Drinking Songs* album titled "Von Rüdesheim nach Aßmannshausen," a paean to the wonders of Rheinland wine. Since it was Sunday and this was a small town, we could find nothing but a camping spot about three kilometers away (possibly the current Naturpark and Camping Suleika to the north) where we could sleep and get food.

We hiked the long way to the camp after stashing our luggage in a hiding spot on the far side of the railroad tracks. We paid the outrageous DM 1.20 to camp there, then bought some beans at the camp store and cooked them on the butane stove. We were kicked out of our chosen spot for some reason by a camper from the Netherlands, so we had to move to a lower level. We borrowed some matches from a Danish camper and got a fire going. There was some kind of explosion and commotion— perhaps more US expatriates setting off fireworks. We slept a chilly sleep.

Monday, July 5, 1971

Geoff fixed us some soup after we woke up early. The campsite charged for the use of their showers, so we decided to forego that luxury for the time being and left the camp with no regrets. We hiked the long way back to where we had stashed our luggage. No one had disturbed it.

As we walked back into Aßmannshausen, we were just in time to catch a bus to the Bahnhof, where there was a train about to leave for Wiesbaden, the capital of the German state of Hesse and the city where Steve's grandmother lived. It was only about 32 kilometers away, so the train took a mere 20 minutes.

We arrived in Wiesbaden and wandered around aimlessly, not knowing what to do, but soon we found a phone number for a youth hostel and located Steve's grandmother's residence. Steve was a bit unsure of himself, so Geoff and I encouraged him to march right up and have a proper visit with grandma. We told him to meet us at the train station tomorrow at 10:00 a.m.

Meanwhile, Geoff and I sat down in the shade in a city park and wrote letters and drank wine and ate carrots. Then we called up the Jugendherberge (youth hostel) at noon to find out where it was, then took a bus, since it was a bit far away. A guy and a girl on the bus were headed there too, so they showed us where it was. We put our gear in a locker and tramped to the Schwimmbad (a swimming pool, possibly the Thermalbad Aukammtal) a couple blocks away. We went swimming for a short while then got out and assessed the girls at the pool, including a blonde Viking Fräulein who was swimming with a kid. We consumed some beer.

Then we went to the market and bought some eggs and cabbage and other foodstuffs, carried it all back to the hostel, and Geoff cooked it in the self-service kitchen around 5:00 p.m. This is when I discovered that Geoff's specialty was Cajun cooking, which requires heavy doses of salt and pepper and any other spices that are handy. His cabbage and sausage came out tasting mighty fine, and I've adopted his habit of adding spice (especially Cajun-style seasoning) to almost any meal. Then we moved into our rooms, which were now ready.

Later we went to a French cellar-style beer place nearby and had a tremendously heavy discussion on Einsteinian physics and its applications to mysticism, drugs, human existence, and UFOs. We came back to the hostel at 9:30 p.m. (because 10:00 was the required bedtime) and talked to a couple American girls. I think that this was the time when two Asian guys asked us if we would like to travel to Afghanistan. Open-minded as we were, we thought this was probably a bad idea. They went over to some girls and made the same proposal, with similar results. I've always wondered what they were up to. We retired to our rooms. The hostel had no showers, so we were glad we had stopped for a swim earlier.

Tuesday, July 6, 1971

We had a nicely prepared breakfast of scrambled eggs, courtesy of Geoff. Then we took a bus to the train station to meet Steve and see whether or not he would be staying with his grandmother for a while. Surprisingly, he was there promptly at 10:00 a.m. He said his uncle happened to be at his grandmother's place and that he would be visiting his relatives in Mainz—just across the river from Wiesbaden—for a while. So, we said our goodbyes to Steve. Geoff and I were somewhat relieved because at times he was a bit of a complainer. He certainly would be better off with his kinfolk instead of vagabonding around with us.

I went to make a phone call to find out what US Army base my friend Dave Hall was stationed at. I did not succeed in reaching Dave, but I did discover that a friend of my father's, John Farrell, was stationed in Wiesbaden at an Air Force base. I called John up and he said to come over at 11:30 a.m. to Lindsey Air Station. He would be waiting in the cafeteria. Lindsey no longer belongs to the Air Force, but since 1993 the area has been home to offices, a high school, and a playing field for the Wiesbaden Phantoms football team.

In the meantime, Geoff had been chatting at the train station with two girls named Sharon and Sandy who were schoolteachers from Tacoma, Washington. By the time I returned, Geoff was getting friendly with Sharon, so he invited them both to go along with us to Lindsey Air Station, where the Air Force employment office was located, to see if they needed any teachers. We started walking the wrong way, then looked at the map and turned around. We finally located Lindsey not too far from the city center, and the nice man at the gate let us through easily because John had told him we were coming.

We were walking to the cafeteria when John drove past and picked us up. He took us to his apartment on the other side of town after stopping for some wurst and pommes frites. We met his wife Ruth and their baby girl who was born in March. We had a feast of beer and wurst while we hashed over old times. John then dropped us off at the employment office in Lindsey. He invited us to the Noncommissioned Officer's Club that night, as he had duties elsewhere at 1:00 p.m.

The Lindsey employment office said we had to go to the main office at Wiesbaden Air Base, so we caught a free military bus to the base, which was way out in the boondocks southwest of the city. We sat around bored while Sandy filled out two application forms for a teacher position. I asked, but they had no hospital jobs. There was a computer technician job available, but Geoff did not qualify for it. We sat around for another two hours then took a military bus to the train station, where we then discussed what we should all do.

Finally, around 5:00 p.m., we decided to walk up to the NCO Club at Lindsey. We put on some buttoned-up shirts and walked to the air station. When we arrived, the officer's club would not admit us, even after we explained that we were supposed to meet John there. They wouldn't even let us into the waiting area of the lounge, so we walked to a nearby pub and had a few beers, discussing educational philosophy and telling dirty jokes.

Then we walked back to the Wiesbaden train station so Sandy could make a phone call. She was apparently still worried about finding a hotel. We all went to another pub, and Geoff and I discussed physics and relativity until we got sleepy and the place closed. Then we went to a park (possibly Reisinger-Anlagen or the Herbertanlagen). I had to walk Sandy back to the train station so she could change her clothes. We went twice because the first time she forgot to bring her locker key. Meanwhile, Geoff and Sharon were making nice-nice in the park. I went to sleep.

Wednesday, July 7, 1971

I woke up in the park in Wiesbaden after about 1½ hours of sleep and walked around until everyone else woke up at 5:00 a.m. Sandy and Sharon had wanted to catch a 5:10 train to somewhere, but they were too late. We saw them off on a train at about 6:00 a.m.

Geoff and I walked to the road that led to Darmstadt and started hitchhiking. Our intention was to visit some cousins of mine on my mother's side who lived in a small town near there. We tried thumbing unsuccessfully for one hour, then we took a two-hour nap. Still a bit groggy, we decided to take a bus to the edge of town, which was a good move. We got a ride from a weird Greek-German guy who was on his way to Frankfurt, but he decided to take us to Darmstadt anyway. He was a terrible driver, going too slowly and not paying attention. He dropped us off at the Darmstadt train station, in front of which was a park where we ate some bread, carrots, and pretzels, and drank some of our last Apfelwein.

At 12:30 p.m., we took a bus to Groß-Umstadt to visit my German cousins. It was a nice ride through fields and forests.

Groß-Umstadt is a sleepy little town on the edge of the Odenwald, where the legendary dragon-slayer Siegfried was murdered by the Burgundian king Hagen of Tronje, according to the *Nibelungenlied*. We located Obergasse 9 (the Johé family drugstore), but it was closed. We went across the street and had a beer and got a free bottle opener with the town's name on it.

Otto Johé opened his drugstore at 1:00 p.m. We introduced ourselves, and Otto introduced us to his longtime employee Sylvia Wieder, then took us upstairs to his residence and introduced us to his wife Elfriede. We talked a lot in German (Geoff was much better at it than I was). Otto gave us a nice grape-limonade mixture that tasted better than American grape soda. On the phone, I talked to my cousin Karl, Otto's son, in Frankfurt, where he was working. The Johés had to run the drugstore, but Elfriede did our laundry and let us take showers. We walked around town a bit.

The Johés took us out for a meal at the Gaststätte und Biergarten zum Lamm. I had an excellent Jägerschnitzel (roast veal cutlet in mushroom sauce—still on the menu in 2023!). The Johés had to travel to Darmstadt on business that evening, so they gave us a ride back to the Darmstadt train station. Otto gave us DM 20 apiece and six eggs and bought our train tickets. We said heartfelt goodbyes.

Cousin Karl Johé met us at the Frankfurt train station around 8:00 or 8:30 p.m. He took us to his apartment in the Griesheim quarter after he stopped off at his friend Reinhard's to make plans for tomorrow. After visiting an Italian ice cream place, we went back to Karl's apartment to discuss politics and decide which one of us would sleep in Karl's one extra bed. We bought some beer for the evening, and Geoff and I flipped a coin for the bed. I won. We went to bed slightly early.

Thursday, July 8, 1971

Geoff and I got up and took showers. Geoff had caught a chest cold yesterday and it was getting a bit worse today. Karl fixed us a breakfast of eggs. We went with Karl to pick up Reinhard and went to a public pool, swimming and sunning and talking about English literature all morning. We gazed wistfully at some beautiful pool Mädchens. After swimming we went to Johann Wolfgang Goethe University's mensa (canteen) for lunch. It was inexpensive and quite good.

We dropped Reinhard back at his place and drove back to the university to park, then walked into downtown Frankfurt. I needed to stop in the American Express office, but it hadn't opened yet. We walked around some shops. I wanted to buy a new backpack, but all of them looked cheaply made and were too expensive. We went to a bookstore, and I bought an *Asterix und Obelix* comic book, quite popular back then, which was about a feisty group of Gallic warriors who are always outwitting the powerful but dim-witted Roman soldiers.

We watched a guy in a downtown Platz (open space) playing piano. He was wearing a top hat and a white shirt that was too small, and he was playing discordant avant-garde music that he had composed himself. When people asked what the piece's title was, he said it was music of the future. Later on, the newspaper reported that someone in the crowd had called the police, who forced him to leave.

Finally, the American Express office had opened, but I found that it did not have the service I wanted. I tried to call the Mitfahrkentralle (ride-sharing place) to see if Geoff and I could find someone going to our next destination, München (Munich) in Bavaria, but I couldn't get through to them.

We bought some peaches at a fruit stand, then went into a grocery store to buy some items for breakfast. We also purchased some beer and wine, then brought the wine over to Reinhard's place, because his wife had invited us all over for dinner. She had prepared a nice repast of hot Ochsenschwanzsuppe (oxtail soup) and ice cream.

Then the five of us went to the movie theater to see the 1970 Jerry Lewis film *Which Way to the Front?* but it was the German version, *Wo, bitte, geht's zur Front?* I was able to make out most of the German dialogue, with the help of Karl and Reinhard's inspired translations. Then we went to a bierkeller for a brew and then back to Karl's. Geoff and I finished off a bottle of

Zeller Schwartze Katz that we had obtained in Andernach. I slept in the extra bed again.

Friday, July 9, 1971

We awoke and had a nice breakfast of eggs, milk, and bread. Geoff and I washed the dishes. Karl had to be at work at 9:00 a.m., so we all went to the Goethe University area early. Karl showed us around the Geography Library where he worked. He said he would call up the Mitfahrkentralle to see what was going on. Geoff and I browsed around in some bookstores for a while, and I bought a few postcards. Geoff bought a physics text and an Isaac Asimov novel.

We went to the proper American Express office, then somewhere else to make phone calls. Geoff lost a few DM due to his unfamiliarity with the phone system, but he went to the post office to complain and, after some red tape and foot dragging, finally got a refund.

Then we walked back to the university to visit the Naturmuseum Senckenberg. There were many fossils (dinosaurs, pterosaurs, and ichthyosaurs) and stuffed birds and mammals on exhibit. We walked back to Karl's library around 6:00 p.m. From his office window we noticed a young couple feverishly making love in an apartment building across the way. "Looks like someone is getting some action," I noted. Fifty years later, Karl told me that was the first time he had ever heard that American slang phrase.

Karl said the Mitfahrkentralle ride was "no way," as he put it. So we went to the Zum Gemalten Haus on Schweitzer Strasse, a little Bavarian café where many locals go to eat. I had a pork rib roast and some excellent sauerkraut, while Geoff had some Apfelwein and bratwurst. Afterward, we had Handkäse mit Musik (stinky cheese topped with onions, a Hessian specialty). As Karl explained it, the "music" (flatulence) comes two hours later. Geoff's cough was getting pretty bad, so tonight we let him sleep in the bed. Karl and I sat up until 2:00 a.m. or so, discussing politics and other fun stuff.

Saturday, July 10, 1971

We had some toast and eggs for breakfast, took some quick showers, cleaned up Karl's spare room a bit, then Karl drove us to an Autobahn ramp outside Frankfurt that would put us on the road to München (Munich). We said fond goodbyes to my cousin Karl.

Geoff and I waited two hours for a ride, while other hitchhikers around us, especially single girls without bras, got rides easily. Finally, a guy named Gerald picked us up in a Volvo 144. Gerald was an attorney and quite interested in the situation in South Africa, but he was in favor of apartheid. He loved beer and wine. He was going to a party with some friends in München who owned a private castle. Along the way, he took us to a small town near Würzburg called Sommerhausen and bought us a bottle of Schloss Sommerhauser Schönlette 1967er Frankenwein—which was excellent. Even Geoff, with his cold, thought it was superb. "We slurped it like hungry dogs," he told me 52 years later.

As we drew near München, Gerald began to boast about the excellent beer and wine available in the city, and he rattled off a million places for us to visit, especially in Schwabing, which is where he dropped us off eventually. Schwabing is a district in the northern part of the city and at the time it was a gathering spot for longhairs and students, comparable to Haight-Ashbury in San Francisco.

We had some beer in an open café there, then we began to ask people in the street about places where we might stay for the night. The Ludwig Maximilian University of Munich was close by, which might afford some opportunities. On our third attempt, we talked to two students whose names were Hans Eugen and Ringard and who spoke English better than we spoke German. They were walking in the direction of the Englischer Garten, a massively large public park where they told us we could probably find a spot to sleep.

They walked us up to the Chinese Tower, where we had some fantastic beer (7 liters = DM 2.20) and some sausage and bacon that Ringard had bought. They were studying at one of the universities in Stuttgart. Hans Eugen was staying in his parents' place in Unterhaching, south of the city center, for the summer. His parents were somewhere else, so he invited us to stay overnight at his family's house.

We took a bus and a tram to Unterhaching, bought some beer, and settled down for some serious drinking and enlightened conversation. Hans Eugen had a nice collection of older 45 rpm records ("Banana Boat," "Marianne," some Beatles, and a jazz saxophonist whose name escapes me now). He asked us if we had ever heard *Die Moldau* (*Vltava*), a symphonic poem by Czech composer Bedřich Smetana, and I admitted that I hadn't. He played it for us, and I was completely blown away. It has remained one of my favorite classical compositions. The music uses tone painting to describe the course of the Vltava River in Bohemia, from its sources as two small springs, through woods and meadows, then through Prague and finally to its confluence with the Elbe River. It's only 13 minutes long, but it packs a powerful punch—suitable for the longest river in the Czech Republic.

Shortly after that, I reached my limit in beer consumption and had to retire for the evening.

Sunday, July 11, 1971

Today I slept late, took a shower, and watched German Sunday morning television for a while. We talked with Hans Eugen and Ringard until 12:30 p.m., whereupon we all went to the train station and rode to the Ostbahnhof (which, incidentally, was celebrating its 100th birthday that year) in München. We then parted with our two German friends, called up a local youth hostel, took a bus to Rotkreuzplatz, and paid for beds in the hostel for two nights. We stashed our gear there. Many Canadians were staying there.

We took a walk down Nymphenburger Strasse and saw all the sights that were to be seen. On Sunday, that did not amount to much, especially since much of it is residential with only an occasional restaurant or store. We wound up walking all the way back to Schwabing, which would have been at least 5 kilometers.

We drank a few beers, then went to the Englischer Garten and the Chinese Tower again.

We met and talked to some Americans who were sleeping in the park, then Geoff and I walked all the way back to the hostel, visiting a poster store and relieving ourselves in a cemetery along the way. We had a couple beers in the Wienerwald pub near the hostel after we got back at 9:00 p.m. There were some kind of odd problems with our lockers.

Monday, July 12, 1971

Geoff and I had a crummy breakfast at the hostel, then we took buses to the Deutsches Museum, the world's largest science and technology museum, located on an island in the Isar River, and had a lengthy visit there. I have a strong memory of also visiting the Alte Pinakothek, an art museum that houses European paintings prior to the 19th century. It is not in my journal, but I think at one time I had a list of the paintings I saw (Dutch, German, Flemish, Italian); now that list is long gone. Perhaps we did go there as well.

We went back to the hostel at 5:00 p.m., where we met a guy named Tom and his girlfriend. We went out for wurst and beers at some restaurant on the Rotkreuzplatz. Around 8:00 p.m. or so, we walked across the street to another place where we got free beers, thanks to a careless waiter. Then we played Scrabble at the hostel with some US and Canadian girls. I won, but just barely. In the middle of the night, we were all awakened by a horrifically noisy thunderstorm.

Tuesday, July 13, 1971

Today it rained all day. Geoff and I split up, he to American Express and other assorted destinations, while I just wandered about.

I took a bus to Munich International Airport, where I searched two hours for a non-existent military telephone and lost all sorts of pfennigs trying, and failing, to contact my friend Dave Hall. Then I caught a bus back to town, walked for a bit, and found a bank and a post office. At the Postamt I tried again to call the American military exchange in Heidelberg. I had to phone twice (more pfennigs lost) because an ignorant, bureaucratic functionary hung up on me. However, I did find out that Dave was stationed at the US Army's Panzer Kaserne post in Böblingen, where he was part of the 5th Psychological Operations (PSYOP) Battalion, a unit of the 4th Psychological Operations Group (Airborne). That made sense because when he was drafted, as I recall, he was able to parlay his writing aptitude into a special job instead of going directly into the infantry.

After rapping with some Americans at the München train station, I walked back to the hostel where we were staying and sat down to read an English-language science-fiction novel I had just bought, Fred Hoyle's *The Black Cloud* (1957), which is about a massive gas cloud that enters the Solar System and blocks much of the Sun's radiation from reaching Earth. Hoyle was a British astrophysicist who espoused a few radical notions, such as his rejection of the Big Bang theory and his theory that life arrived on Earth from microorganisms and viruses in outer space, distributed by cometary dust—the panspermia hypothesis.

Geoff returned to the hostel with a girl named Debbie, who was interested in Sufism. I was completely bored with the topic, but I accompanied Geoff and Debbie to a nearby wurst place for a meal. They wanted to travel downtown to a club. I really did not want to go with them, so instead I went back to the hostel and got some sleep. Geoff and Debbie discovered that their club was too expensive or crowded or closed or something, so they came back to the hostel. When they returned and woke me up, I discovered that someone had stolen all of my paper money. Uh-oh.

Wednesday, July 14, 1971

Geoff and I took a bus to the edge of München and began hitchhiking to Stuttgart. We met another hitchhiker from Ceylon who wanted to be an auto mechanic. (It was only one year later that Ceylon became a republic and changed its name to Sri Lanka to repudiate its former status as a British dominion.)

We waited perhaps an hour, then we got a lift with a man driving a minivan who also picked up the Ceylonese guy and another thumber from Denmark. He gave us a nice ride all the way to Böblingen, about a two-hour drive, letting us off at a spot that I thought was only 1–2 kilometers from the Panzer Kaserne base, but it turned out to be a bit further.

Geoff and I walked for a while until some GIs in a Volkswagen bus that had passed us going the other way turned around and gave us a ride all the way into the base, sharing and smoking some hash in the process. Panzer Kaserne was originally a German Army base built in 1938 and primarily reserved for tank regiments. Legend has it that Adolf Hitler gave a speech at the Nazi officer's club building and that experimental tank improvements were tested at the base. The US Army took it over in July 1945.

We walked through the main gate without any hassle and went into the 5th PSYOP Battalion headquarters, where Dave should be. We talked to the sergeant major, the senior non-commissioned officer, who went and got Dave for us.

Dave came and greeted us, walking with a cane. He said he had broken his leg in a practice parachute jump the day before. In reality, as I discovered in 2022, his injury was from a night parachute jump in April 1971, after only three weeks "in country," less than 10 miles west of Can Tho, Vietnam, related to the Chiêu Hồi (Open Arms) propaganda leaflet program. The 5th PSYOP Battalion was dropping these leaflets from low-flying helicopters, often while they were being fired upon. The propaganda encouraged Viet Cong or North Vietnamese soldiers to defect to South Vietnam.

Dave and some other soldiers parachuted into the area. He was tasked with checking on the viability of some ground-mobile audiotape devices that spread a continuous audio message encouraging desertions. These had been dropped at strategic positions in the country, accompanied by abundant leaflets, which were also safe conduct passes. Once these were set up, the commandos would be picked up at designated retrieval points.

However, Dave mistook a road beneath him for a river, landed badly with his parachute, survived the night under extremely dangerous conditions, and was airlifted out the following morning with a shattered patella, femur, and other broken bones in his right leg. He was taken to a Navy medical ship, where he was fitted with a temporary prosthetic appliance and sent first to Hawaii, then stateside for more surgery. When he was sufficiently patched up, he went back to the base at Böblingen, later spending several weeks of rest and recuperation in L'Estartit, Spain—which is why he knew so many people there during our visit later on.

Dave was not the in best condition to go on a two-week leave. He set us up in the barracks while he went to the hospital for an evaluation. I could not communicate very well because the hash I'd smoked in the VW bus had gotten to me. A soldier named Leonard took us over to the snack bar, where we got some American food (banana split, 35 cents). Geoff and I had some difficulty finding our way back to the barracks. We sat outside for a while, contemplating America's military might, then went inside.

Dave returned and told us that despite his broken bones, he thought he could take some leave time in a couple of days. We watched some soldiers playing baseball. Geoff felt sick or tired and wanted to rest, so Dave and I went to the NCO–Enlisted club to discuss old times in Columbus, Ohio. We came back and picked up Geoff and went to B.G.'s room to smoke hash and listen to music tapes. Sam and Mac were also there. Geoff smoked a bit too much. We thought about seeing a movie at the base, but Geoff was still feeling too uneasy to go. I went and rapped with Dave and Murray about foreign countries, then went to sleep in an Army bunk.

Thursday, July 15, 1971

Geoff decided to leave today because he was feeling homesick and not up for any more exotic adventures. But first we walked into Böblingen to the IBM Germany Research and Development offices, and I waited and read *Der Spiegel* while Geoff talked to the human resources people, only to find out that there were no jobs available (although they had already made him fill out an application). This took until 11:00 a.m.

Then we went to a bakery and bought some bread, and I said goodbye to Geoff, who was going to hitchhike to Stuttgart to catch a train.

I went back into town and then into the nearby woods for a walk. I went to a restaurant called the Waldheim—no longer in operation in 2023, but formerly located at Heuweg 1—for a beer (DM 1.30) and walked around quite a bit more in the woods and discovered old (wartime?) lookout towers. I found a dead mole.

I came back to the base and read. Dave came around 3:30 p.m. and we watched soldiers playing cards for money. I went to Dave's barracks and watched him pack for our trip. We went to the NCO club again at 6:30 p.m., then went to see the Robert Redford movie *Little Fauss and Big Halsy* at the base theater, but it was so-so. Went to bed shortly afterward.

Friday, July 16, 1971

Dave went to work again this morning. For no reason at all, I decided to walk in the direction of Calw, a town in the Black Forest about 22 kilometers away. It was farm country all the way. I bought some fresh peaches at a small town, then walked about 9 kilometers or so to a place I called Schlafhausen in my diary, an even smaller town with nothing in it except some old houses. Made it there by 12:00 noon. (Since there is no place with that name currently in the vicinity, it may actually have been Aidlingen or somewhere else nearby.)

I hitchhiked back with some businessman who took me into Böblingen, where I went to the bank, ate some ice cream, walked around aimlessly, and took a nap in the park. I visited the post office and mailed some letters, then walked back to the Panzer Kaserne base. There was some news going around there about a girl who had been decapitated—only her head was found, and her body was gone.

I met Dave when he got off his assignment at 3:30 p.m., but we had to wait for the NCO on duty, named Joe Acosta, so that

Dave could get his leave slip approved. We watched a military baseball game again until 5:00 p.m., when Joe approved the leave slip and we started on our journey.

Murray and his girlfriend Inge gave us a ride to the Stuttgart train station. It was a long ride because it was during rush hour. We took a train from Stuttgart to Heidelberg, then walked along the Neckar River in a city park where we were to meet Dave's friend Ray, who was stationed there at the Patton Barracks, and some other people.

We finally found them—Ray, J.B., T.C., Pancho, and a few girls. They had been smoking some weed. We smoked what they called a "Heidelberger" (from what I recall, this was a large joint made up of some choice cannabis) and a couple bowls of hash there in the park. The experience was enhanced by listening to some rock music on Ray's tape player.

We watched the barges being towed along the Neckar and saw Heidelberg Castle getting illuminated for the night. Ray, Dave, and I went over to J.B.'s place for some more cannabis and listened to *4 Way Street*, the new live album by Crosby, Stills, Nash, and Young. J.B. eventually got wiped out, so Ray, Dave, and I went back to the park to sleep. I was "tripping on my childhood," according to Dave, which probably means I was reminiscing about growing up in Gettysburg, Pennsylvania. We had a very good night's sleep in the park.

Saturday, July 17, 1971

When I woke up, Ray had gone to pick up J.B. After he returned, Ray drove us north (about an hour) to Frankfurt so that Dave could check on his motorcycle. We smoked some hash and ate breakfast along the way. Ray drove us directly to the home of the Army friend who was storing and repairing Dave's cycle—a 1942 German Army 500cc BMW that he had bought from a former Wehrmacht mechanic who served in Nazi-occupied Croatia. The cycle wasn't completely fixed yet, so we smoked some more hash and Ray drove us back to Heidelberg.

Ray sold me his Army rucksack for $5, so that I wouldn't need to buy a new backpack right away. He dropped the two us off on the Autobahn 5 southbound around 2:00 p.m. so that we could start hitchhiking to Switzerland, although Dave and I were receptive to altering our plans if the circumstances of our journey compelled us to go in another direction.

Our first ride was in a crowded Volkswagen bus that took us about 30 minutes to Bruchsal with two other thumbers. We got another ride shortly afterward with two French soldiers and sat crammed in the back of their orange Opel, all the way to Baden-Baden, about 65 kilometers. Then we got another good ride for about an hour and a half with a German couple to Mulhouse, France, not far from the point where the borders of Germany, Switzerland, and France intersect. We had wanted to continue in Germany so we could proceed directly to Switzerland, but what the heck. They dropped us off at the Gare de Mulhouse, the train station.

We ate an inexpensive French meal, then we walked to a field a few meters away (possibly the Square Géneral de Gaulle) and camped out. It was a bit damp.

Sunday, July 18, 1971

Dave and I woke up and it was raining hard. We got our gear and ran to two large, unused sewer pipes where we sheltered. A derelict was hiding out there too. He bummed 2 francs from me.

At this point we decided to go to Spain, where Dave knew a nice seaside resort called L'Estartit. He called it a "British tourist colony," where it wouldn't be hard to find English-speaking people. As I discovered many years later, Dave had spent several weeks of R&R there several months earlier for his shattered leg that he injured during a parachute jump in Vietnam.

We waited until 7:45 a.m., then we walked to the station and found out that a train would not be leaving in the right direction until 9:00 that night. We decided to hitchhike instead, but first we enjoyed hot chocolate, a buffet, and eggs somewhere.

We asked a local Frenchman for directions, but we must have looked quite confused, so he gave us a ride to the edge of Mulhouse on the road to Belfort, a town to the southwest. We waited an hour before we got a short ride with a French guy halfway to Belfort. He dropped us off on a lonely stretch of road.

Two other groups of hitchhikers were picked up almost immediately, but we waited 3½ hours in the rain for a ride. Three Moroccans finally gave us a lift into Belfort. We attempted to hitch a ride in town for hours with absolutely no luck, so we bought train tickets for 109 francs. Meanwhile, we went to a restaurant near the train station for an expensive meal with an impolite waiter. Dave had wurst and a salad. The people here seem a bit snooty and distrustful of strangers.

We waited a long time for the train and took naps until it finally arrived at 10:17 p.m. We stumbled into a compartment that was already occupied by a Moroccan guy who said he wasn't going to sleep, but he did anyway. We passed through Besançon and Bourg-en-Bresse, where some French soldiers boarded. We went to sleep shortly after passing through Lyon—a beautiful city on the Rhône River with well-lit streets and magnificent architecture.

Monday, July 19, 1971

I woke up off and on through the night, then became fully conscious by the time we got to Montpellier near the Mediterranean coast. There the landscape got a bit hilly and began to look more Spanish.

The train arrived at Portbou, Spain, where Dave and I went through Spanish customs and boarded another train with a different track gauge. This one was quite crowded, and we had to stand up all the way. Two Spaniards, one with a belt made of US quarters, began singing some songs that sounded like flamenco music but, looking back, may well have been examples of local *rumba catalana.*

We arrived in Girona, Spain, around 10:30 a.m. The bus to L'Estartit would not arrive until 12:45 p.m., so we bought some bread and lemonade and sat down to a feast after we converted our currency at an American Express office. We drank some carbonated Spanish beer at an outside café, and Dave went off to buy some cigarettes. The people here seemed very friendly. Girona is a scenic locale in northern Catalonia, with an ancient cathedral, medieval fortifications, and other sights that we did not have time to pursue.

It began to rain heavily, but we soon caught a bus to L'Estartit on the Costa Brava. In 1971 this was a splendid tourist destination, although its charm has apparently dwindled somewhat since the 1990s. Nonetheless, it is still a popular spot for scuba diving, especially around the Illes Medes, a craggy group of islets just offshore. The town has preserved many of its pre-war fishing houses and cobbled streets, giving it an antique charm cherished by those seeking escape from the miasma of modernism.

Dave slept most of the way on the bus, but I saw some nice scenery. In L'Estartit, we wandered over to Kim's Bar—still operating in 2023—where there were some British hippie types who knew Dave's friends, Mac and Betty. They told us how to get to the Beachcomber Bar where another friend, Eddie, could be found, but Betty had just left for London the previous Friday.

We went to the Beachcomber Bar and met Eddie and George, then walked around town looking for a room. Our quest was futile. Dave ran into some other acquaintances, Dave and Graham and Pete, at the El Cisne. We went to the Santana twice to find a room, but a Spanish woman there told us, "Non segundo" (no second) or something like that to indicate either that she had no vacancies or couldn't accommodate two people.

We dined at the Fisherman's Bar—I had chicken, Dave had a hamburger. Later, the affable Eddie let us have a barely furnished room upstairs from the Beachcomber Bar for 65 pesetas a night. There was no mattress, so we had to use our sleeping bags. We visited the Cove, an area of the beach where at one time Mac had apparently camped out a couple of nights. We met Kate, whom I described as a "hell-nymph" in my diary, but don't ask me why, because I have no memories of her at all. A French family was also at the Cove.

Dave and I discussed the Spanish Civil War and Las Vegas on the way back to the Beachcomber Bar. We had some snacks and drank some beer, then went to bed. There was loud music coming from the bar until it closed.

Tuesday, July 20, 1971

Dave slept in, but I got up at 8:00 and read for a while. Later we went somewhere on the beach and picked up a "breakfast" for 15 pesetas that consisted of a roll with butter and a cup of coffee. Dave was disinclined to look for a better place to stay. I decided to go climb a hill outside town, which Dave could not do because of his injury.

While I was gone, Dave walked around town with his acquaintance Graham and swam at a place where a few people were scuba diving. Dave said it looked like Bodega Bay in California (where Alfred Hitchcock's 1963 film *The Birds* was filmed) where the rocks stretched all the way to the water with no beach.

My hill was rugged, but I conquered it. It took a while to ascend because I didn't always follow the prescribed GR 92 footpath. A bunch of tourist families, some British, some German, were climbing along the easy trails. There were many grasshoppers and lizards and dragonflies and large birds. At the top, I looked down on a fantastic view of the sea and the town.

The descent on the other side of the hill was laughably easy. I decided to walk towards the Cove to see what was on the far side of it. The terrain was quite rocky for miles around. I viewed a Coast Guard tower encircled by an electric fence and surrounded by magnificent cliffs that dropped straight down to the Mediterranean and were approachable only by boat.

"Almost mad with fever," as I exaggerated in my diary, I scrambled back to town and had a couple beers at one of L'Estartit's many bars. I bought a wine skin for 150 pesetas, then located Dave at the Beachcomber around 5:00 p.m. He was drawing sketches of people. (I wonder what happened to them?)

We went for some dinner at the Lamar Bar, and I had some excellent chewy cuttlefish. We stayed out drinking at the El Cisne and the Beachcomber. We ran into Kate again, so it turned out that she was a real person and not a vision. We also met Graham and had a good time. Then we went to a bookstore where Dave bought Patricia Welles's adaptation of the screenplay for the 1969 film *Bob & Carol & Ted & Alice* (translated into German). We looked around in curio shops for cheap stuff and found some inexpensive clothes (which I didn't buy).

We attempted to go for a swim at the Cove, but the waves were too treacherous, with much white water and an abundance of sea urchins. We went back to the Beachcomber and talked to people, notably three tourist girls who came in after we did. Later on, we took showers and went to bed.

Wednesday, July 21, 1971

At 8:00 a.m. we got up, intending to go hiking, but found that we couldn't leave because the Beachcomber bar doors were locked until 10:30 or so, trapping us inside, and the proprietors, Eddie and Len, were asleep. Dave went back to sleep while I read. We finally were liberated at 10:30, so we went to breakfast somewhere for an omelet. Dave's leg was acting up, so he thought he'd better not go hiking.

I hitchhiked 3 miles west to just outside the town of Torroella di Montgrí so I could climb a hill where there was a 13th-century fortification, Montgrí Castle. I ascended through terraced fields, finally reaching a somewhat steep and rocky incline that led to the top of the hill, the Montgrí Massif. After a moderately grueling climb, I achieved the summit by 12:30 p.m. The castle was incomplete and was merely a square affair with circular towers at each corner. After exploring it, I followed an easy path back to Torroella and came across a strange stone monument-like structure with an archaic cross on top—apparently a cistern.

Then I visited the massive old Catholic church in town, the Església de Sant-Genís, which was built from local limestone between 1306 and 1609. Its two towers are an odd couple, one an octagonal square without a roof, and the other a pyramidal hexagon.

I found a ride back to L'Estartit with a Walloon couple, then located Dave at the Beachcomber at 2:00 p.m. He had gone swimming at the beach and come back to the bar to do some sketches. We heard some Basque singers. It started raining heavily after we went to the El Cisne—a veritable torrent with horrendous thunder and lightning that dumped about 6 inches on the ground. The electricity went out.

After the deluge subsided, we went back to the Beachcomber and took a siesta. Then we walked over to the Lamar for some food. Dave had spaghetti and I had a hake dish (hake is a European fish like a cod). It was the best meal I've had so far in Europe. After stopping back at the Beachcomber, we went to Alice's discothèque, then back to the bar and to bed. Loud music again erupted from the Beachcomber bar below.

Thursday, July 22, 1971

Dave slept in this morning, while I read. We crept out of the Beachcomber at 11:00 a.m. Dave's leg was feeling a bit better, so he decided to go hill climbing with me. It was a long, rugged climb that was a bit challenging for Dave, but he made the hike stoically, unflinchingly, and manfully. Braving thorns, treacherous rocks, and poisonous insects, we struggled to the top of a nearby hill overlooking the Cove. Then we hiked down an easier path back to town and made it back by 2:00 p.m.

Thanks to our stroll, Dave's leg was now in worse shape. We mailed a few letters, then took a dip in the Mediterranean Sea and hung around the Beachcomber for a while, drinking and playing cards (rummy or gin rummy) until 6:30 p.m. We were both feeling the need to hit the road again, perhaps to Morocco so we could add another continent to our itinerary, and we ate our last L'Estartit supper at the Lamar.

Dave had the hake this time and I had some halibut, which wasn't quite as tasty. We roamed around a lot then went back to the Beachcomber and to bed.

Friday, July 23, 1971

We got up at 6:30 a.m. to catch the 7:30 bus to Girona, the nearest city, about 45 minutes away. Unfortunately, Dave forgot to bring his cane, which might hamper his future mobility a bit. We bade a silent farewell to L'Estartit as we bought some lemonade for the ride. Dave got some extra sleep on the bus.

The bus driver let us off somewhere near the Autopista (freeway) outside Girona, but not quite close enough, as we had to walk about 2 kilometers to get to what turned out to be the wrong (northbound) exit. Then we found the correct southbound exit where there were already two Dutch guys thumbing. They were continually fooling around, holding up wine bottles as cars passed, and other silly stuff. One of them was always wandering around, not thumbing, while the other guy was talking to us, mostly dooming our chances for a ride. Around 1:00 p.m., they decided to leave and take a train to Barcelona.

Fifteen minutes later we got a ride from a young Spanish lawyer who expounded on Spanish politics and history the entire way to Barcelona. He was quite entertaining. He said he used to be a communist when he was a student but gave it up because he had to cooperate with Francoist Spain's fascist regime to make a living. He dropped us off in the northern suburbs of Barcelona at a subway station.

We took the subway to Liceu station and walked to the Plaça Reial, which is where a tourist agent lady had told us a bunch of Americans would probably be. The square had many restaurants and outdoor vendors, so we bought some *horchata de chufa,* a tiger nut drink popular in Spain that is made from the edible tubers of a plant in the sedge family (it tasted oatmeally), along with a big liter of beer.

I went in search of people who might be going to Morocco, while Dave stayed with the luggage. I came across a few

Americans who said it was easy to go to Morocco, but you had to look like you were going to spend money. They also said we would have to get a cholera inoculation at the border because an epidemic had broken out there.

Then I talked to Alice and Janet and another American girl who were all attending school in Barcelona. Alice wanted to go to Morocco too, but she didn't have a ride. She gave me her phone number in case I found one and said she would be at the American Express office the next day at 10:00 a.m. The girls steered me in the direction of a student travel bureau. I found it, but it was closed until 4:00 p.m. I wasted 30 minutes talking to an English dude who also said it was easy getting to Morocco—no hassle at all, man— but he had to catch a ride back to London because he had received a telegram from his mum telling him to "Return at once."

I posted an ad on the bulletin board at the student travel bureau saying that Dave and I could be reached at the Hostel Roma. Then I went to the American Express office. I found some people who had been looking to take riders to Morocco, but they had just filled their quotas. No one else was going. I talked to an American couple who said that the ferry to Morocco from Algeciras, Spain, required that we have both a car and a haircut. Our prospects were looking dim.

I went back to where Dave was, and he told me he had discovered that our destination, the Hostel Roma, was all filled up. We had another beer. We wandered around looking for a place to stay, then it started raining.

We passed by a Spanish kid on a street corner who asked us if we were looking for a room. He took us to his family's Pensión Nuria and we were able to stay there for 60 pesetas per person per night. The guest house was run by his Mama, a jovial but all-business extrovert whom we instantly liked. The hot showers there felt good.

Dave and I got some dinner at a restaurant, then we walked around after dark and saw a replica of Christopher Columbus's galleon, the *Santa Maria,* in Barcelona Harbor. This ship had been built for use in a couple of Spanish films and left on display as an attraction. I found out years later that it was damaged by Molotov cocktails thrown by a Catalan independence group in 1990 and dismantled. We had a couple beers, then went back to our serendipitously found pensión.

Saturday, July 24, 1971

Dave and I decided against going to Morocco because there had been a failed attempt to overthrow King Hassan II only two weeks earlier. That, as well as the cholera and the insects and the police and other nuisances. Switzerland was our next choice, home to dairy cows, chocolate, the Alps, and red-vested yodelers with feathers in their hats. Dave went to a bank to change some currency, and we visited the American Express office at 10:00 a.m., but Alice wasn't there like she had promised.

We went to a market of sorts and bought chocolate cookies, wine, and what we thought was lemonade but was really mineral water. We went to a park and drank it, but it tasted like camel piss. From there we walked back downtown and paid the Pensión Nuria people 120 pesetas for another night. Bought some new film for the camera and drank a big, hefty beer.

We wended our way to the Barcelona Museum of Contemporary Art. On the way, we took photos of some tricorn-hatted Guardia Civil officers and the Christopher Columbus Monument, a 197-foot-tall edifice built in 1888 to remind everyone that the Italian navigator had returned to Barcelona after his first voyage to report to his Spanish funders, Queen Isabella I and King Ferdinand V, both of whom are enshrined on the monument's pedestal, along with other dignitaries and a group of stately lions.

The art museum was about to close, so we went to the Barcelona Zoo instead. We tried calling Alice, but our pay telephone wasn't working properly. At the zoo we saw some Przewalski's horses and Père David's deer and penguins (not in a cooled environment) and the zoo's famous albino gorilla, Snowflake, who was about 7 years old at the time, having been captured in Spanish Guinea (now Equatorial Guinea) at the age of 2. Snowflake became famous when *National Geographic* put him on its March 1967 cover. He is still the world's only known albino gorilla. He was euthanized in 2003 after he developed painful skin cancer due to his condition. The zoo also housed many birds (emus and ostriches and crowned cranes and condors). We saw elephants and hippos and zebras and tigers and leopards. We also saw a Spaniard riding around on a horse, but he wasn't one of the zoo's denizens.

We stayed at the zoo until 6:00 p.m. closing time, whereupon Dave returned to a store and bought a leather coat he had put a down payment on earlier. We rapped with some hippies who were camping out near Barceloneta Beach. After walking around and buying dinner at a market (bread, meat, cheese, and watermelon) we went back to the Plaça Reial and called Alice again. She said a friend was coming into town soon, but we all could maybe do something tomorrow if we called Janet at 10:30 a.m. the next day. We had another big frothy beer at the Plaça Reial.

We were unaware that tonight was a Barcelona festival night, and the square was impressively crowded with revelers. Dave and I discussed literature then went back to the pensión. We gave half the watermelon to Mama, who was delighted.

Sunday, July 25, 1971

Dave and I both slept late until 9:50 a.m. We called Janet at 10:30 but she could not get together with us today. We decided not to stay another night at the pensión, so we broke the news to Mama. We took our gear and walked to a park, where we watched a military pageant in honor of some colonel or admiral.

We went to the Barcelona Museum of Contemporary Art again and strolled around for a long time. It mostly had obscure Spanish impressionists, but there was also a Miró and three Salvador Dalis. We viewed *The Battle of Tétouan* by Marià Fortuny and a weird astrological painting called *Genesis* by Josep Gumí Cardona. There were many nudes.

Afterward, Dave and I walked to where we thought we would find a beach but there wasn't one. We walked down many streets but still couldn't find a beach. We walked back, found the beach, lost it again, found it again, but there were no Americans sunning themselves there, only Spaniards. We drank a couple of orange Fantas and walked around looking for a bus. We finally found one that took us to the Autopista. We thumbed for a couple hours.

Finally, a family came along around 8:00 or 8:30 p.m. and gave us a ride north to Premià de Mar along the N-11, a local route that followed the coastline. It was dark by now, so the hitchhiking was bad. Some police came up to us. They were very friendly and told us politely to move away from the intersection, so we did. Still no luck at getting a ride, so we walked back along a road leading to the Autopista. Still, no luck.

Two girls found rides after standing with their thumbs out for no more than two minutes. We hoofed it 2 kilometers to the Autopista, but there was very little traffic. It was time to camp out off the side of the road where there were snails, ants, funny plants, a pleasant smell, and bats!

Monday, July 26, 1971

At 5:30 a.m., I woke up and found there was absolutely no traffic on the Autopista. Dave arose at 6:15 to the same situation. We decided to head back to the N-11 route along the coast through Premià de Mar, where at least there would be plenty of traffic. We walked back, grumbling all the way. Dave went to buy something to drink, but I couldn't hitchhike while he was gone. As soon as he came in sight on the horizon, I put out my thumb. We got a ride less than one minute later from a chubby Spaniard on his way to Girona. Along the way, we passed by a horrible auto wreck and saw a Romani camp. The driver entertained us with some quaint Spanish drinking songs and love songs. He let us off in Girona around 9:30 a.m. I accidentally left my new wineskin in his car.

We waited on the near side of Girona for 2–3 hours, then walked through town to the other side, where we found many hitchhikers. We walked down the road to a bar where we met either a French or English couple, I'm not sure which. A German shepherd dog had stolen the woman's shoe. We went back to the road but had shitty luck, as there were many clusters of thumbers.

While waiting under a bridge, we saw a car with Trieste stickers. (I'd heard of Trieste from my days as a stamp collector.)

We were hot, tired, thirsty, and disgusted. We walked to a shopping center and asked people at souvenir shops and gas stations if they could give us a ride. At about 3:00 p.m., we had some luck with two Germans who said they could take us to Lunel in southern France, which turned out to be a good five-hour ride. They were friendly types. They bought some peaches somewhere, which we ate along the way. We compared the German and American armies.

At the French border we got some cholera information. There were many weird wooden things along the French coast, which may have been related to erosion or the fishing industry. We saw the low, rolling hills of Provence and some quaint French villas. The Germans let us off in Lunel around 8:30 p.m.

We bought beer, cigarettes, and food in this very friendly town with narrow streets. We met some French thumbers who gave us some bread they got for free at some store. We walked to the edge of town and found a field with a wall around it that looked to be a promising place to camp out. We went to sleep, but around 11:00 or 12:00 p.m. we were woken up by a guy who was looking for a friend he had split up with about 100 kilometers back. He joined us for the night behind the wall.

Tuesday, July 27, 1971

Dave and I woke up, ate some food, then walked back into Lunel. At 7:15 a.m., we got a ride with a French guy to Nîmes, about 30 minutes away. We talked to a German hitchhiker in Nîmes who advised us to walk down the road to a "better" place. We had no luck. Two girls got a ride almost immediately, of course. A gendarme approached our location and started directing traffic right in front of us. He stopped a few cars for making illegal turns or other minor infractions. We couldn't hitchhike while he was around. Who wants to pick up someone when there is a gendarme two feet away?

We walked down the road again and ran into a fellow thumber we had met in Girona. We were all stationed at a fruit stand, having no luck, cursing the heat. Our friend told us there was a better place down the road about 2 kilometers. We tried to work an Esso station, asking people gassing up whether they could give us a ride, but the owners kicked us out. We kept trying with no luck until 3:00 p.m. Dave and I had a long, unflattering conversation about French people.

We joined a Moroccan chap named Muhammad who had been standing along the side of the road for 25 hours. Muhammad was also traveling to Switzerland (like us), so we decided to go to the nearest train station because we were getting nowhere. We took a bus to the Nîmes train station. Muhammad was talking to a girl, telling her how terrible the French were. We found the station, then walked three or four blocks to a bank, because the train station apparently did not have a place to change currency. I walked around trying to find a place to buy a good map of France, while Dave and Muhammad had a beer somewhere. Muhammad decided to travel only to Lyon, where he would again try to hitchhike. We all took the same train, which left at 4:24 p.m.

Muhammad was very intelligent; he had studied philosophy in school and was reading Albert Camus in French. He listened to a lot of American music—Woodstock, Procol Harum, even Frank Zappa. His father was a printer who specialized in maps and lived in a town near Rabat. He kept emphasizing how inexpensive Morocco was and how terrible the French are. He left our train at Valence.

Dave and I started seeing some Alps around then. We arrived in Grenoble, along the Isère River, where there were some splendid views. I talked to two girls from Montreal, Quebec, who claimed they had degrees in nursing but did not behave like they were older than about 17. Dave didn't even bother talking to them.

We arrived in Geneva, Switzerland, around 10:30 p.m. and got off the train. We had some beer and bread at a café near the train station. Since this was the French part of Switzerland, the service was poor. The waiter seemed to be insulting our intelligence. We walked to a park along the Rhône River and tried to sleep, but there were too many people. We walked to the huge

Parc des Eaux-Vives near the edge of Lake Geneva and camped out. Ants decided to make a nest in my backpack.

Wednesday, July 28, 1971

I cleaned the ants out of my backpack. Dave wanted to take it easy this morning, so I let him sleep while I walked all the way back to the post office to mail a letter. I returned at 9:00 a.m. and woke him up.

We walked down to a market and bought some bread and a kind of chocolate spread to go with it, as well as some apples and lemonade. We sat with a view of the famous Jet d'Eau on the lake and ate our meal, marveling at the fountain's speed and power. Its two pumps shoot 150 gallons of water per second some 460 feet into the air throughout the day and into the evening.

We trekked a long, long way to the outskirts of Geneva to go to our next destination, wherever that might be. Some girls got a ride right away. Dave and I were picked up after 45 minutes by a Swiss guy who was driving to Lausanne, less than one hour distant. He owned a boarding house where some people from Chicago were staying. He had studied commerce in school and served in the army for three weeks a year. He bought us some beer in Lausanne, then took us to a spot on the road leading to Bern where there were no other hitchhikers.

We got a ride right away from a woman in a Volkswagen going to Fribourg in Switzerland—although at first we thought she was going to Freiburg im Breisgau, Germany. She spoke excellent English. She showed us around Fribourg a bit—it was a beautiful city on the cultural border between French-speaking and German-speaking Switzerland with a medieval city center and a splendid Gothic cathedral. Dave said it reminded him of Calw, near Böblingen.

We found a thumbing spot on a winding hill road looking down on the town. Before long, we got a ride from an Italian truck driver who took us to the near side of Bern, a little more than an hour away. We had no luck there, so we took a bus to the far side of town and found the road to Luzern.

It started drizzling. We walked a short way, then thumbed. A lady passing by told us there was a better spot up the road. We walked to the spot, where there was a cigarette stand. We waited about two hours as it began raining heavily. A fräulein behind the desk at the cigarette stand made a sign for us that said "Luzern."

Then our luck instantly changed. We were picked up by a Frau Affolter, who said she could take us to her place at Kriens, which must have been more than 100 kilometers away, just outside Luzern. She invited us to sleep overnight in her laundry room. She told us that her son Heinz had told her to always pick up hitchhikers.

Frau Affolter was a motherly type who showed us all the scenery along the way to Kriens, like houses decorated with flowers, and old roof paintings, and a covered bridge (very Pennsylvania Dutch–like). We started getting into the real Alps at this point. We got to her place around 7:30 or 8:00 p.m. We took showers, and Frau Affolter made us some excellent homemade Swiss soup and sausage with rice. She owned an old dress closet dated 1823 that she had refinished and repainted herself. We met her husband, Werner Affolter. We watched some Swiss TV that had Donald Sutherland on it and watched the news. Her place was very nice and middle-class. I went to sleep after rolling my sleeping bag out on a fold-out plastic bed in the laundry room.

Thursday, July 29, 1971

Dave and I got up at 7:00 a.m. because Frau Affolter had to go to work. We ate a breakfast of bread and butter and marmalade and milk. I was feeling spunky and decided I wanted to do some alpine climbing, so she gave us some tips on how to climb up Mount Pilatus, a series of peaks overlooking Luzern. Its highest peak, Tomlishorn, is 6,289 feet tall.

We set out to tackle the mountain at 7:45 a.m. We started hiking on the wrong path; Swiss Wanderwegs seem to be terribly marked. It was rugged and slippery going up the first steep slope. Dave decided he could not go any further because of his leg injury, so we parted, and he said he would take a cable car and meet me at the summit, whenever I got there. The aerial cableway station was conveniently based in Kriens, so he did not have to go far.

I scrambled back up the slope and crossed a big field. I took a rest and ate some peaches and bread that Frau Affolter had given us. It was a long, confusing path up, not well marked. I saw cows and mist and heard the tinkle of cowbells. It was a fantastically thick alpine forest. I finally arrived at the Bandweg path around 11:30 a.m. after wandering around on different trails. I tried to tackle it, but it was just too steep and confusing and slippery for me. It almost required climbing equipment.

At this point, I spilled some milk in my backpack and completely ruined my camera and many of the rolls of film I had taken. I crawled back down the slope on all fives (including my butt) to an interim stop where I could board the cableway to the top, which was a lower peak—the Esel, I think. Somehow I got on the lift for free. I met Dave at the summit, and we feasted on chocolate in the restaurant area.

We took a 40-minute easy route to the Tomlishorn peak. There were caves there and plaques where people had died. It was very sunny at the top. Then we returned to the observation platform and the summit restaurant. Dave told me he had gotten to the summit at 8:45 a.m. or so. He had walked around on all the well-paved paths, had a beer for 2.5 francs, and shared some bread with a Japanese tourist.

Dave and I took the cable car all the way back down, which took about 30 minutes. We caught a bus into Luzern, where we saw some swans and ducks and gulls on the River Reuss. We walked across the Kapellbrücke, an iconic covered wooden footbridge (the oldest in Europe) with many triangular paintings in the archways that dated from the 17th century.

We found a bookstore, but I still could not locate a map of France. We had some beers in a café and discussed the futility of human evolution. We watched as some sight-seeing American girls walked right into a Swiss teenager who was riding a bicycle. We left the café after further discussing philosophical matters.

We bought a bottle of French red wine (Dijon 1966) to take back to the Affolters, then we caught a fast bus back to their home at 2 Zielweg in Kriens at 6:30 p.m. to be in time for dinner. Frau had made some spaghetti for us, so we had that and our wine and some of our hosts' Swiss light red wine—all very good. We watched the latest reports on the TV news about the Apollo 15 astronauts (Scott, Irwin, and Worden) who were making their final approach for a fourth lunar landing. Then we watched a German documentary on sleep, dreams, and hypnosis, where students had been voluntarily deprived of sleep for four days. We started watching a French program on UFOs, but we got sleepy and went to bed.

Friday, July 30, 1971

This turned out to be a BAD DAY.

We arose at 7:00 a.m. Frau Affolter made us some bread for breakfast. We said heartfelt goodbyes and gave our sleeping mat to Frau for her son Heinz to use when he hitchhikes. We walked down to the bus stop, with Mount Pilatus cloudless and majestic in the distance. We snuck onto the bus with phony tickets that we acquired somewhere, but we were caught and fined 5 francs. We bought a legitimate ticket and boarded a bus that we thought was going to the train station, but it was traveling in the wrong direction. When we realized it, we got off the bus. We tried to get on a bus going in the other direction for free, but we got caught and had to pay for another ticket.

Around this time, we gave up on the train station and decided to take this bus all the way to the edge of town where there were a bunch of people thumbing. Our destination was now Heidelberg, where we could connect with Ray and some of Dave's other friends. We tried moving to the front of the line to hitchhike, but it was just a bad hitchhiking spot, so we walked up the road a fair distance to a forested area where there was a truck lay-by. We had no luck whatsoever. We tried both with and without using a cardboard sign and stood there for three whole hours.

Finally, a German guy came along and took us to Neuenkirch, only about 10 kilometers northwest of Luzern, where we bought some beer and bread and chocolate. Then we walked to the far edge of town and again had no luck for a very long time.

Another German stopped and offered us a ride, but we declined since he was only going to Sempach, a mere 2 kilometers down the wrong road. We hiked ahead to a lumber yard where there was a place where cars could pull over.

Many drivers were headed for a swim in a nearby lake, the Sempachersee. No one would pick us up. We were just about to walk further when a hippie in an Esso uniform gave us a ride to Sursee on the far side of the lake. By this time it was 4:00 or 5:00 p.m., and there was no way we could make it to Heidelberg by nightfall. We walked down the road to a gas station.

At this point, I suddenly discovered that I had lost my passport somewhere, which meant I could not cross the border into Germany. Bummer! We were stuck at the gas station for only 30 minutes before we got a ride to Zofingen with two liberal types who had a stereo tape player in their Citroën. After a ride of 20 minutes or so, they let us off at a good Autobahn intersection with traffic going two different ways to Basel, which is where I thought I could get a new passport.

We got a ride shortly afterward with a guy who Dave thought was driving nearly all the way to Basel. However, it turned out he was only going a short 15 minutes away to Olten, and we got let out at a terrible spot way out in Swiss Nowhereland. By this time, we were deflated, discouraged, and somewhat paranoid.

We finally flagged down a friendly Swiss man who took us to a Basel suburb (perhaps Muttenz). He talked about many things, especially the area around Basel and its wondrous sights. When we arrived there, we took a bus to the city center and tried to call the US Embassy, but guess what—there was no embassy in Basel. They were only in Bern and Zürich.

One of the reasons we were going to Basel was so that I could connect with Madelaine Hirt, an exchange student that my Aunt Helen and my cousins knew, who lived in the city. Unfortunately, I did not have her phone number. We found Nadelberg strasse, where she lived, all right—it wasn't too far away. We knocked on the door at 15 Nadelberg, but Madelaine's roommate said she had gone to India a week ago for a six-month trip. She gave us Madelaine's sister Gabi's address, who lived just around the corner. It was a bit too late to bother Gabi, so we stumbled to some café where we had some non-alcoholic beer. I ordered a beefsteak and some French fries, while Dave had something else. We also had some Pepita, a popular Swiss-made grapefruit drink with a parrot on the label.

After it got dark, we went out and gazed at the Rhine River and talked about our youth and smoked a cigar and a cigarette. We found a very small park near the offices of Sandoz Ltd., the pharmaceutical company that first sold LSD as a psychiatric drug from 1947 to the mid-1960s. We thought this would be a splendid place to sleep.

At one point, the police came around and asked to see our passports and money. After laughing at something in my wallet, they went away, saying "Gute Nacht."

Saturday, July 31, 1971

At 4:30 a.m. I woke up and tried to rouse Dave. That was an impossible task, so I bedded down again. I got up again at 7:00 a.m. and wandered to the post office, which opened at 7:30. There I mailed some postcards and phoned the US Embassy in Bern, which told me that if I could be there on Monday I could get a replacement passport quite easily. The call only cost 50 centimes.

Dave and I went to a bakery and got some bread, then to a meatery and bought three kinds of meat; both stores were at a quaint little place called Martinskirchplatz, near St. Martin's Church.

Dave decided to return to Germany while I went back south to Bern to get a new passport. He would take a train to Freiburg im Breisgau, which did not leave until 11:10 a.m. I put my stuff in a train station locker and walked toward the Basel Zoo, stopping first at a camera and electronics store. I picked up a zoo brochure and read it in a café while I drank a Warteck Lager, a full-bodied light beer brewed in Basel.

Then I returned to the Bahnhof because I forgot I had wanted to give Dave $100 so he could buy me a reel-to-reel tape recorder at the army base exchange store. However, I got there just in time to see him off. He said he would try to take the train all the way to Heidelberg, even though he only had a Freiburg ticket.

I went to some bookstores and bought a Stadtplan (city map) of Basel. Then I walked to Gabi's flat and met Gabi, who fed me some apricots and strawberry juice. She was very intelligent and spoke French. Her dog's name was Pasha, but she was trying to find another home for him. She owned lots of books—Rudolf Steiner's *Theosophy,* Timothy Leary's *The Politics of Ecstasy,* and a book of Salvador Dali prints, *Dali über Dali.* She also had many excellent rock, jazz, and classical albums—Jimi Hendrix at the Isle of Wight Concert, Spooky Tooth, Pink Floyd, Janis Joplin, Otis Redding, Jerry Lee Lewis, lots of J. S. Bach and other Baroque composers. We talked about Madelaine and Basel and her life and my life. She had just bought a new African rug for her flat. She worked in public relations, supplemented by freelance writing and some design work for a leather goods company.

Gabi advised me to go to the city art museum in the afternoon while she visited a Canadian friend. Tonight we could perhaps go to a macrobiotic restaurant for dinner. She told me to come back at 7:15 p.m.

After buying some food for tomorrow, I walked to the Kunstmuseum Basel, one of the best art museums in Switzerland and the oldest public art collection in the world, dating back to 1661. I gazed at dozens of old Flemish and Dutch masters as well as impressionists (Manet, Monet, and Cézanne) and cubists and Swiss artists like Arnold Böcklin, Paul Klee, and Ferdinand Hodler.

I washed up at a gas station and returned to Gabi's place at 7:15. Her Canadian friend Cleo came over. She had just been to Glastonbury. The dog Pasha was getting frisky. Our French-English-German mixed conversation was getting a bit confusing. I had some pastiche (nut rolls) and a trendy French-Swiss drink made from all sorts of spices, including anise; it tasted a bit like fermented licorice.

We talked and took Pasha for a walk, then went to the macrobiotic restaurant. It was a musical venue, and there were lots of people there whom Cleo and Gabi knew. We smoked a little bit of hash and stayed there a long time. Actually, I began to get bored. Had some mandarin orange tea and rice and a mixture of fruit and grain that was quite good—it might have been muesli, although that tends to be a breakfast meal. On the way back we discussed the pros and cons of LSD use.

I had not been invited to stay at Gabi's place, so I left to sleep in a park near the train station, possibly De-Wette Park, and got to sleep around 1:00 a.m.

Sunday, August 1, Swiss National Day, 1971

I was awakened at 5:00 a.m. by the city police, who told me to vacate the park. I stumbled over to the Bahnhof and continued to doze on a bench there.

Eventually, thanks to the Stadtplan and a schedule, I discovered how I could get to the edge of town by bus and immediately took one there. Luckily, I didn't have to thumb for very long before I got a nice ride with Herr Herz and his son, who were both quite friendly.

Herz was a 60-year-old Swiss businessman who was going all the way to Murten (a town west of Bern) by way of Biel, Lyss, and Aarberg, a total of about 75 miles. He pointed out some interesting things like farmhouses, a memorial obelisk, a tobacco field (yes, families have farmed tobacco in western Switzerland since the late 16th century), and Mont Vully, a vineyard-covered hill near Murten.

We talked about the Murtensee (also known as Lake Morat), since they were headed there to go swimming. They owned a spot on the beach where they could put up a beach tent. They finally talked me into going with them. Herr Herz treated me to a Kaffee at a café in Murten, a beautiful small town that was founded in the 12th century.

At the lake I met Helen (Herr Herz's daughter) and her friend Hans-Ulrich. We went swimming in the Murtensee, which is the warmest lake in Switzerland, because no icy water from the mountains feeds into it and it is shallow and easily warmed by the sun. The Herzes are a very nice family. I helped them pack up their tent afterward and they took me out for a beer and bread and wurst at a nearby café.

Herr Herz dropped me off at an intersection outside Murten, where I got a ride within 30 minutes. It was an Italian guy from Milan who lived in Bern. I was the first hitchhiker he had ever picked up, because up to that point he had been a bit wary of them. He said I should visit Florence, Venice, and Rome if I ever got to Italy. He said he was traveling to California in one week to see some friends. He let me off at the Bern city center at 3:00 p.m.

I wandered around looking for a youth hostel. I finally found one, but it didn't open until 6:00 p.m., and it looked a bit expensive, so I walked to the Bahnhof and talked to a Japanese guy for a while. I took some photos that I would need for my passport at an automated photo booth, then I bought a city map of Bern and set off to find a park near the American Embassy. I indulged in beers and meringue with whipped cream at a nearby café. I walked to the Bern Zoo for a short visit and located another park that would be good for sleeping.

The city was hosting Swiss National Day ceremonies on the other side of the swiftly running Aare River, but it was a long hike to find a bridge. The festivities included a brass band, a large bonfire, official oratory, and the national anthem. Here and there people were setting off apparently illegal fireworks. It seemed exciting enough to me, but the locals seemed slightly bored. An official fireworks display took place from 9:30 to 10:00 p.m.

I stumbled back to my hiding place in the park and slept until 1:00 or 2:00 a.m., when a thunderstorm broke out. I hightailed it to a bench where trees shielded me from the downpour. I dozed a bit until the rain stopped, then walked back to the hiding place at 4:00 a.m.

Monday, August 2, 1971

This morning I slept until 8:00 a.m. Walked through the Bern Zoo again and arrived at the American Embassy at 8:30. The automat photos I had taken yesterday were not good enough for the passport, so I had to hike back to the train station (and got a bit lost on the way) to spend 14 francs for five official passport photos, which weren't ready until 11:10 a.m. Many stores were still closed because of the Swiss National holiday, but I bought some fruit at a market, then picked up my photos.

I took a quick bus back to the Embassy and got everything straightened out, except that the place closed for lunch at 12:30 and the passport wouldn't be ready by then. So I went to a café by the zoo and had some "Spaghetti Tierpark" with mushrooms and pieces of beef and cheese. Afterward I met a New Yorker—a schoolteacher and student from the Bronx—who had also lost his passport. We walked back to the Embassy together, talking about NYC problems, different underground magazines, and Revolution in Amerika. We got there when it reopened at 2:00 p.m. It took another hour to get the passport, which cost me 50 francs.

Then I hopped on a bus to the outer edge of Bern. I arrived at a hopeful spot at 3:45 and waited only two minutes before I got a ride with two Americans (Jeff from Birmingham, Alabama, and Tom from Boston, Massachusetts) all the way to Freiburg im Breisgau, Germany, about a two-hour drive. Jeff had bought a German Volkswagen in Düsseldorf and had been in Europe for about seven months. He was going all the way to Luxembourg in two or three days and was working at Sperry-Univac Germany as a computer programmer. He had picked Tom up hitchhiking in Paris, and together they had driven to the Riviera and the Alps. Tom got a bit sleepy from the French red wine we were drinking. Both were anxious to see American girls again when they returned to the States. We got stopped briefly for some reason at the German border in Basel.

Jeff said he had picked up an American hitchhiker on the Autobahn who told him that, "Gee, that town called Ausfahrt must be a huge place—I've seen signs for it for the past 50 miles." Ausfahrt means "exit" in German.

Jeff let me off at the Freiburg exit. I waited a while until all the other thumbers got rides. I tried without using a sign and got a ride with Wolfgang and Maria, who were going to Rastatt, or somewhere near there, about 70 miles to the north. They were very nice and invited me to stay at their place that night. That was fortunate, because there were many hitchhikers at the Rastatt exit.

Wolfgang and Maria (and their 4-year-old daughter Miriam) were in the process of moving to Freiburg. Wolfgang taught and studied philosophy, while Maria was studying education. Their house was filled with posters, copies of *Der Spiegel,* and art prints of famous Modigliani, Brueghel, and Van Gogh paintings. Books were everywhere, photos of Sophia Loren and Moishe Dayan, moon photos, old maps, etc. They gave me a meal of sandwiches, grapefruit, pickled asparagus, milk, and red wine mixed with mineral water.

We watched the Apollo 15 astronauts walking around on the Moon on TV. Astronaut David Scott was performing an experiment with a hammer and a feather to validate Galileo's theory that when there is no air resistance, objects fall at the same rate of speed due to gravity, regardless of their mass. After dinner, we had a big, long discussion about US and German domestic policy and problems, especially East Germany. We talked about World War II and the different conditions in West and East Germany. Maria served as a translator when necessary. We chatted until midnight. Then I slept in a wonderfully soft bed.

Tuesday, August 3, 1971

When I got up at 7:30 a.m., Wolfgang was already up. He said he had trouble going to sleep in the summer, and he had stayed up last night until 4:00. We had a breakfast of bread and quark (curd cheese) and tomatoes and coffee. Wolfgang and Miriam then drove me to the nearest Autobahn entrance. I gave Miriam my *Asterix and Obelix* comic book because they were so kind.

Some French army guy was at the Autobahn ramp doing something or other that made me uneasy. However, after 15 minutes I got a ride from an older, near-sighted man from Zürich, Switzerland, who was driving to Rotterdam in the Netherlands. He let me off at Karlsruhe, only about 26 kilometers away, because the road to Stuttgart branches off there to the east, and I was headed in that direction to go back to the Panzer Kaserne in Böblingen to meet Dave after he returned from Heidelberg.

Soon I got a ride from a mild-mannered, bearded German student who was going to Stuttgart. He either had a speech impediment or a bad chest cold. He let me off on the road to Böblingen, where I got a ride to the base with two freaks in an Opel Blitz truck.

I walked onto the base and found that Dave had not returned yet. I met up with Dave's friend Manzek, and we went for a drive and a smoke. To pass the time, I walked to the snack bar and got a soda, then hiked to the Waldheim in Böblingen and had a beer and pretzels. I took a siesta for a while in the woods, then went back to the base at 5:30 p.m. to check for Dave, but he had still not returned from Heidelberg, so I walked back into Böblingen and ate at the café near the Bahnhof and had a couple beers. Came back to the base after reading Fred Hoyle's *The Black Cloud* some more. I got there at 9:00 p.m., but still no Dave.

I waited until 10:30 when he finally came in, dripping wet because it was raining. Melvin came over and talked with us.

Dave told us the story of his adventures since Saturday. The conductor had noticed he did not have the full fare to Heidelberg, so he had gotten off the train at Freiburg and hitchhiked with a German guy. They had a good talk until the car went kaput and he let Dave off at a shitty exit. Dave finally made it to Heidelberg, where he played frisbee and swam in the Neckar River. He found out his motorcycle would still not be ready until next Saturday.

Melvin brought some wine over and we talked about UFOs. Cooper came over to say hello. After a while, I crashed on an empty army bunk.

Wednesday, August 4, 1971

I arose and took a bus to Stuttgart at 7:30 a.m. to visit the Staatsgalerie (art museum). It was only about a 15-minute ride and the museum would not open until 10:00, so I just walked around for a while. I bought some food, then went to a bookstore and purchased a two-volume paperback edition of the *DTV Atlas zur Weltgeschichte* (1964) by Hermann Kinder and Werner

Hilgemann, a fascinating atlas of world history from the Stone Age to the present. It had hundreds of colorful maps depicting migrations, invasions, explorations, and revolutions; a concise explanation of political events, philosophical and religious ideologies, and technological developments; informative flow charts that showed the administrative structure of governments, including the United Nations; and pie charts identifying the composition of legislatures. I kept those volumes for many years, even after I bought an English translation published by Doubleday in 1974, which I still own.

In the art museum, I focused on its collection of 20th-century art (Picasso, Miró) until noon. Afterward, I sat for a while in a park where there were some fountains and a statue of Eberhard I, Duke of Württemberg (1445–1496), perhaps my remote ancestor. The statue is now on the grounds of the Altes Schloss history museum. Called Eberhard the Bearded and generally well-liked, he unified two parts of the County of Württemberg and made Stuttgart the capital. Although largely a positive influence on local history and culture (he founded collegiate churches and had many Latin texts translated into German), he was responsible for expelling Jews from many of the towns, something I can't forgive him for. However, a decree banning them from the entire duchy did not take place until 1521, well after his death. Also, his only legitimate child, a daughter, died in infancy, but he had other children by single women and, apparently because he was such a popular prince, they were officially legitimized as if they had been born in wedlock. Thanks, granddad!

It was only in 2021 when I posted on Facebook a color portrait of Eberhard the Bearded next to a photo of me (when my beard was reddish) that I realized there is indeed a family resemblance.

I stayed in the park a long time, reading my new atlas. In a buffet restaurant, I had some beer and wurst. Then I paid DM 2.20 to take a bus back to the Panzer Kaserne base. I met Dave at 5:30 p.m. and we gathered up our laundry and found a ride to the Patch Barracks in Stuttgart with, I think, Doug. We did our laundry at Patch and at the exchange there I gave Dave the money to purchase an Akai reel-to-reel tape recorder that Dave will ship to me, courtesy of the US Army. Dave said it was the best model to get because it was built well enough to withstand the heat and dampness of Vietnam.

We rode back to Panzer Kaserne with some soldier who I thought was insane, although I don't remember why. We looked around for B.G. and Cooper, who had just snitched a reserve parachute. We went to B.G.'s place and smoked and talked, then we hiked down to the Waldheim, smoking hash along the trails as we made our way through the dark forest. We got there around 11:00 p.m. for beer and schnitzel, then walked back to the barracks.

Thursday, August 5, 1971

It was getting to be time for me to return to England, as I needed to make sure that Seaglair would provide me with an airplane ticket back to the states. But first I wanted to visit Dave's friend Ray again in Heidelberg and spend a day in the city. Dave tried to find me a ride to Heidelberg but couldn't. I bade him farewell and got a ride to the Autobahn ramp with a German driving a Citroën.

When I got there, I made a makeshift sign, and a hippie in a bus picked me up and took me somewhere not too far away. Then it wasn't long before a German truck driver stopped. It was a splendid ride all the way to Heidelberg, a good 75 miles away. The driver talked a bit too quickly for me to understand him. He let me off at the wrong exit because I had misread my map.

I walked through the industrial sector of the city, then bought some bread and cheese at a bakery, drank a Coke, and had a feast. I made my way to the Patton Barracks in the Kirchheim district where Ray was stationed and hassled with the MPs at the gate, including one Sgt. Schumacher. No one seemed to know where Ray worked. I was able to get Davis to sign me in, but Ray was nowhere to be found.

Discouraged, I went to someplace called the Grundhalle for a beer. At 4:30 p.m., I got someone else to sign me into the Patton Barracks again. Finally, I found Ray, who was in his billet. He was on "sick call" and confined to his quarters all day, apparently a common ploy that the soldiers frequently used to get out of daily assignments. It seemed to be tolerated by the duty officers, at least up to a point. We talked for a while, then I located Rocky.

We all drove over to the Neckar River and found Rocky's friends Pancho and Bruce. We played frisbee in the park and had some beer. We took Bruce with us over to Joey's, but Joey wasn't there.

After dark, we went up to the ruined yet iconic Heidelberg Castle and smoked some weed within the arched balconies of the Glass Hall. The sight was spectacular, with the castle and the picturesque pedestrian bridge (built in 1788) across the river all lit up. We got very high, and Rocky started reading some of his poetry. We left after a long, enjoyable time and drove over to Joey's again. He still wasn't home, but we ran into him a little bit later and went in and smoked a bowl of hash. Everyone played Hearts (the card game) except me because I was a bit too stoned. I crashed in Rocky's quarters back at the barracks.

Friday, August 6, 1971

Rocky decided to go on "sick call" today, but it took until 9:30 a.m. or so for him to get approval from the duty officer. We met Ray, who was also "sick," and went to get my passport back from where it was deposited at the front gate. There was a slight hassle in retrieving it, but I managed to overcome the bureaucracy.

I went to the train station to pick up my luggage, which I had apparently stored in a locker at some point. Then Rocky drove me to the Autobahn entrance. I waited there for quite a while as other people—Italian guys and two Americans—got rides. I finally found a ride to Frankfurt, about an hour away, with an American of Puerto Rican descent. He dropped me off at an entrance ramp for the Bundesautobahn 3, which would take me to Köln.

This spot was a hitchhiking desert with no one stopping whatsoever, even though there were no competing thumbers. I tried another exit, but still no luck. By this time, it was 1:30 p.m. or so, and I was quite thirsty. I would give anything for a Coke. The nearby presence of the Rhein-Main Air Force Base, adjacent to Frankfurt Airport, was no help in finding a ride.

I trekked over to the Airport Hotel for some bread and drinks, which made life a bit more enjoyable. I tried yet another Autobahn entrance, but a clump of thumbers was stationed there. No luck again, so I took a nap by the side of the road. When I woke up, I found many of those people had gotten rides, including the guy adjacent to my spot. I began silently cursing the cars that drove by. A couple of girls were thumbing in front of me, and someone stopped for them.

But I cleverly strolled past the stopped car and the two girls asked the driver if he had room for me. He did. The girls were Karen and Marcie. Marcie was studying education at the University of Washington in Seattle. Karen was quite good-looking and was from Pennsylvania. They were headed to Amsterdam and were very friendly.

The German driver let us all off at a shitty exit near Wiesbaden, but Karen and Marcie snagged a ride and took me along with them. A German truck driver let us off at Limburg after a half-hour drive. We tried hustling some rides at a gas station there. The girls found a ride with a guy going to Rotterdam, while I got a ride from a truck driver who was going toward Siegburg. I never saw Karen and Marcie again. Oh well, that's life.

My truck driver was quite nice and gave me a bunch of lemon bonbons to take with me. He let me off at an excellent spot near Koblenz where all sorts of Dutch truckers were stopped. I had just started thumbing when a girl named Greta ran up to me and asked if I would like some tea. I said sure, and she took me over to meet Kumal, a Turkish truck driver, and Helmut, who was hitchhiking with Greta from Austria. We had some Turkish tea and a wonderful time listening to Kumal playing his lute-like instrument—probably a *saz*.

Kumal was driving all the way to London. He hesitated taking on another rider, but he said he could take me to Köln. It had begun to rain, so I said that would be fine. Perhaps that was a big mistake, for Kumal took me way past an appropriate exit to a crummy little stop on the side of the wrong road. I had to walk a long 5 kilometers to get to a better road. I was too tired and it was

too late to hitchhike, so I sacked out in the underbrush. It started
raining again at 4:00 a.m.

Saturday, August 7, 1971

At dawn I arose and started thumbing, with no luck,
naturally. I decided to walk down the road to see if there was a rest
area, but that was another big mistake. I had to walk some 6–7
kilometers to even get to the next exit. I found it at 6:45 a.m. and
started thumbing.

Soon I got a ride from a nice German who was going to
Duisburg, about an hour away. He told me he would switch cars
there and then proceed to Amsterdam, where he had plans to go
sailing. He dropped me off at an exit near Duisburg, where I stood
for an hour and a half with no luck. It started looking like rain
again. The cars going past did not look remotely encouraging.

At this point, I began to get weary of hitchhiking all the
time, so I walked 3–4 kilometers to the train station in Duisburg
and purchased a ticket for a train to Amsterdam, a nice long ride
over the flat countryside. I dozed on the train and sleepily got off at
Utrecht by mistake. I roamed around aimlessly for some minutes
before I figured out that I could use the same ticket on the next
train to Amsterdam, which I did.

The city was wondrous and welcoming—there were many
hippie types (American, German, Dutch, English) everywhere.
Unfortunately, there were no available lockers at the Amsterdam
train station to stash my gear. I called Kris Gilpin (who had been
on our New York to Gatwick flight) but could not connect with her
because the woman who answered the phone did not speak
English. I saw some calliopes somewhere, probably near the
Amsterdam Centraal train station. I purchased a map of the city
and wandered around, had a beer or two, then decided to find a
park where I could sleep.

On the way, I found out that Daan did not live too far away,
so I decided to go there first, as it was nearly 6:00 p.m. (Daan may
have been another exchange student who my aunt had
recommended I look up, but I do not remember.) The city had all

sorts of quaint curio shops, used bookstores, and dark cafés. I found Daan's place, but no one was home. Then I went to a Jewish restaurant called Shoarma and had salted mackerel and rice.

Next, I wandered a long way to find a good place for a beer. I located one and sat there for a long time because I was very tired. I decided to say goodbye to Amsterdam and return to England right away.

The train station was not far away, so I walked back and bought a ticket for a train to Zeebrugge, Belgium, at 8:30 p.m. It took every ounce of will power I could muster to refrain from asking the train station attendants, "Pardon me boys, is that the Zeebrugge Choo Choo, on track 29?" But somehow I managed.

I slept most of the way, but I had to change trains at Brussels. The Zeebrugge train did not leave until 6:00 a.m., and I had to walk to the South Station because the Central Station was closed. I overheard some English dude telling his wife how annoying the French people in Brussels were. I slept in the station until 5:00 a.m. or so.

Sunday, August 8, 1971

After I woke up, I found out from a ticket agent that, in order to get to Zeebrugge, I would have to change trains again in Bruges. So I decided to just stay on the first train, which was going to Ostend, and take a ferry from there. The train left at 6:00 a.m., and I had a hard time keeping my eyes open. The conductor woke me up at Ostend, where I bought a ticket for the ferry across the English Channel, which left at 9:50 a.m. I sipped some coffee at a café there and browsed through my *DTV Atlas zur Weltgeschichte* before boarding the ferry at 9:30.

It started to get crowded very quickly, but I found a place on the side of the ship, reading and sleeping and getting kicked inadvertently by passersby for the next three hours. Finally, I saw the White Cliffs of Dover, signifying the land of Matthew Arnold and King Lear. I disembarked and decided to hitchhike to Canterbury after I had a look at Dover Castle.

First, I got something to eat at an American-style cafeteria I stumbled across. As I walked through town toward the castle, a man named John pulled up next to me and asked if I wanted to buy a car. I said no, but he insisted I wait a bit and talk because he was also an American, from Wisconsin. We chatted for a while as he gave me a ride to Dover Castle, and he explained his situation: He had to leave the UK unexpectedly and did not have time to sell his car in a normal way. I finally offered him £10 for his car, a steel-gray 1956 Austin A35.

We walked around the castle as he considered my offer, viewing armor, guns, the keep, the chapel well, and other sights that you might expect to see in a medieval fortress. John hesitated, then went back into town to talk to some kids on bicycles and a guy at a garage, attempting to get a better price. He couldn't, so he came back to me. I said my offer still stood, except I had to check on auto insurance tomorrow.

John and I went to the White Cliffs Hotel on Dover Beach, where he was staying. He introduced me to his wife Janet and his daughter Jennifer. Then I walked to a restaurant where I got a nice meal of sausage and chips for 25p or so and afterward walked down to the ferry station to cash some traveler's checks. The man there told me where the Automobile Association (AA) was in town, so I went to their offices and inquired about buying insurance and untangling whatever red tape there might be involved in purchasing a British car. Then I walked back to the White Cliffs Hotel and told John that he had a sale.

The old Austin A35 had to be started by sticking a rod into the motor and hand-cranking it—perhaps because the battery was low. John helped me practice driving, as I was scared shitless about driving on the left side of the road and shifting gears on a somewhat antiquated auto. I said goodbye to John at 7:45 p.m. or so, then decided to drive off to Canterbury. But first I went to the AA and bought one month's insurance for £6. Then I pointed the car northwest and made several wrong turns.

I picked up a hitchhiking couple named Pete and Mary, who wanted to go to Oxford. I said I could take them all the way to the other side of London, forsaking Canterbury, but I warned them about my cautious driving abilities. Pete was a very pleasant chap.

We discussed religion, British and American politics, drugs, and other normal subjects. My gear shifting was a bit grindy, but I had gotten the hang of it almost by the time we got to London.

We drove through London around 11:00 p.m. Pete provided the directions and worked the turn signals while I concentrated on driving and watching traffic. I dropped them off on the northwest side of London on a road that went to Oxford. I cranked the car up again and drove around looking for a parking place, finally finding one by the side of the road where there were a few abandoned cars.

I went to sleep in the car. It wasn't very comfortable, but I got used to it. A pair of curious policemen woke me up at 3:00 a.m. to see if anything was amiss. No problem. They were quite friendly blokes.

Monday, August 9, 1971

I remained in the car snoozing until 8:00 a.m., then drove down the road to an Esso gas station in Southall. (It may have been the very same one that is still there in 2023 off a roundabout on Ruislip Road, but I'm not certain.) I left the car there after the manager said he would take a look at it and try to figure out why it was having trouble starting. In the meantime, I walked to the Southall railway station, which was nearby, and took it to the London Victoria underground terminal in Westminster.

Here I saw the real city of London for the first time in all its bustle and glory. I wandered down Victoria Street looking for the Seaglair Corporation office, which was supposed to handle my return flight. I passed the red-and-white-striped brick Westminster Cathedral with its steeple looking like a factory smokestack.

I located Seaglair, and the people there said they would confirm my reservation on a flight to the US, possibly to Niagara Falls, Canada, for September 9. I could find a domestic flight back to Columbus, Ohio, from there. I needed to return to Seaglair by September 2 or 3 to pick up the ticket.

I walked to an American Express office on Haymarket Street to convert some currency, took a shortcut through St. James's Park—a beautiful mass of greenery, smack in the middle of one of the largest cities in the world, with its lake and small colony of pelicans. On the other side of the park, I saw some horse guards riding down the mall in all their 18th-century finery.

Nearby, I viewed the 138-foot-tall Duke of York Column next to Waterloo Gardens and the Royal Society. Completed in 1834 with the duke's statue on top, the column celebrates King George III's second son, who led the British Army during the French Revolutionary wars.

Then I walked away from the Mall and passed through the Admiralty Arch to Trafalgar Square and the 169-foot-tall Nelson's Column, completed in 1843, where the old boy who died so heroically on the *HMS Victory* (which Steve and I visited in Portsmouth on June 26) gazes majestically over the city, the empty sleeve of his amputated right arm inconspicuously pinned to his jacket.

I located an American Express mail office, hoping that my father had sent me a letter or two, but it was crowded, and a guard suggested I come back in 30 minutes. So I went to a small café where I got a big meal of meat pie, lamb, chips, salad, and tea. I returned to American Express and discovered there was no mail for me. I got another traveler's check cashed at Barclay's Bank, then went to the post office to call my father—collect. I got in touch with him at 1:00 p.m. or so and we chatted for a while, and I asked him to send some money to the London American Express office to tide me over for the rest of the month. He was glad I hadn't been captured by scoundrels or fallen into the English Channel or seduced by countercultural anarchists. He never had much disposable money, but I promised him I would pay him back later (and I did).

Then I decided to stroll in the direction of the British Museum. I passed by the National Gallery, the huge art museum in Trafalgar Square, then I walked up Charing Cross Road and saw innumerable used and new bookstores that I suddenly felt compelled to browse through. I found an occult bookstore and purchased a poster, a book on LSD for my landlord Ron in Columbus, and a new book on yetis by Odette Tchernine.

In another bookstore, Watkins', I bought a copy of the Penguin edition of the 1967 postmodernist novel *Gog* by British novelist and historian Andrew Sinclair. I had read the US edition in 1970 and became somewhat obsessed with it. It's about a tall man who washes up on the coast of Scotland and cannot remember who he is. The only clues are two tattoos on his hands, one reading "Gog" and the other "Magog." He wanders around Scotland, England, and Wales, trying to discover his identity, and meets all sorts of weird individuals along the way, many of whom he perceives as mythological beings or characters in British folklore. It's not for everyone, especially in the 21st century, and it is riddled with obscure literary references. But the style and story were similar to the novels of John Barth and John Fowles, and I appreciated its archetypes and landscapes enough that I began annotating my copy. More on this later.

I thought to myself, I am really liking London. I walked past Soho to the British Museum, but I discovered that its library was open only to users with a declared research topic. I walked south on Whitehall and saw a few government buildings, the parade ground for the Horse Guards, and the Palace of Westminster next to Big Ben. I took a quick saunter through Westminster Abbey, where I saw the burials of many former Poets Laureate.

It was starting to get late, so I walked back down Victoria Street to Victoria Station and took the train back to Southall. The Esso people said that my car needed both its battery recharged and a new starter motor. The new motor would cost almost as much as I paid for the car (okay, that wasn't so much), but I decided to postpone that.

I sat outside and read until it got dark, then I went back to the car, which I had moved and parked in a small, dead-end lane called Cressage Close. I read some more and went to sleep, hoping the nearby residents wouldn't notice or mind.

Tuesday, August 10, 1971

I woke up in the car, feeling a bit cramped, and worked on this diary until 8:00 a.m. when the Esso station opened. I took the car in to get the battery charged, then walked north to Northolt, where I went to a chemist's (drugstore) and a café for an English breakfast. There is a London Underground station in Northolt where I bought a Red Rover ticket that allowed me to take buses all day.

I took the tube to Victoria Station, then caught a bus to the National Gallery, which I had walked past yesterday. However, the museum did not open until 10:00 a.m., so I strolled over to the National Portrait Gallery and looked at its Centenary Photo Exhibit, which featured images by British photographic pioneers Henry Fox Talbot and Eadweard Muybridge. I had heard of Muybridge and his galloping horse, but I wasn't familiar with Talbot, who invented both a way of stabilizing photographic paper so that images would not be overexposed and a developing process that reduced the required exposure time in a camera.

Then I had a hankering to visit the offices of *Flying Saucer Review* magazine, a respected periodical among ufologists, which I had been subscribing to since 1966. I took a long (more than half an hour) bus ride to Peckham on the other side of the Thames River. I stopped in a pub and had a pint of Watney's Special Bitter and asked where King's Grove street was. They told me, but I went to a bakery and a fruitery first.

I found 49a King's Grove, but it was only a flat, not an office. It was probably where one of the editors lived, but it looked like no one was home. I bussed back to Charing Cross, where I paid a second visit to Watkins' Bookstore again and bought three UFO books, one of which was *The Warminster Mystery* by Arthur Shuttlewood. I purchased a handy map of the UK at another place.

By this time it was 3:00 p.m., so I went to an Italian restaurant and had a pizza for 32p. Then I took another bus to Hyde Park and strolled around. I scrutinized the statue of Achilles, a tribute to the Duke of Wellington (the victor of Waterloo) that was made in 1822 by Sir Richard Westmacott using 33 tons of bronze from cannons captured in Wellington's campaigns in France. The park was peaceful and induced many contemplative thoughts as I took a long, leisurely walk past its many fountains and two lakes, watched some rowers, and marveled at the multitude of dogs.

I walked through Kensington Gardens and sat on a bench for a while. People were flying kites. To get back to the Esso station in Southall, I had to take innumerable buses and made the best use of my Red Rover ticket. Before picking up the car, I talked to a 9-year-old boy who said he was lost. Despite the freshly charged battery, I still had trouble getting the car up and running. I drove to the Red Lion Hotel in Southall, which had a pub, sipped a Watney's Red Barrel, and read until 11:00 p.m. I drove to a quiet lane nearby and slept in the car.

Wednesday, August 11, 1971

Around 8:00 a.m. I woke up and had some trouble hand-cranking the car to get it started. A man parked nearby walked up and asked if he could help with his battery cables. He did, and it worked wondrously. I decided that things could not continue like this, so I drove to a garage in Alperton about 5 miles to the northeast. I told the mechanics to put in a new starter motor, which they said would cost me £9.

Then I took the tube to the Natural History Museum in sunny South Kensington (as Donovan called it on his *Mellow Yellow* album). I had to wait until 10:00 a.m. when it opened. The museum has excellent fossil exhibits with all sorts of ichthyosaurs and plesiosaurs, many casts and original dinosaur skeletons, ammonites, crinoids, trilobites, and brachiopods of every description. There was an excellent display of fossil hominids, including Louis Leakey's 1969 find of an *Australopithecus boisei* skull at Lake Turkana in Kenya. I saw giant fossil fish on display, as well as mammals, birds, reptiles, amphibians, insects, and corals. The meteorite section was good, although they could have had more on exhibit, because the museum owns more than 2,000 samples in its collection. There was a fragment of the Cold Bokkeveld carbonaceous chondrite that fell in South Africa in 1838. The museum has a vast mineral collection, but I lacked the time to see all of it.

I called American Express, but they had not yet received the money transfer from my father. I commuted back to the

Alperton garage and picked up my car. It started up right away, which was a good sign. I decided to go for a test drive, so I went about 4 miles to Northolt and ate and read at a café until 5:00 p.m. Then I drove haphazardly westward through Uxbridge, Denham, and Iver Heath, then south to Windsor, Ascot (past the famous racetrack), Bracknell, and west of Aldershot in Hampshire, where I parked by the side of the road and took a leisurely hike through the woods looking for a place called Caesar's Camp on my map. I never did find it (I mused that he might have taken it with him when he left). However, it is only an unmarked open space on a hill with a lake and a single bench. In fact, it probably has little to do with Julius Caesar at all and is essentially an Iron Age hill fort that preceded the Roman Republic by many centuries.

At nightfall I drove north to Bracknell in Berkshire and drank warm beer in a pub until 10:00 p.m. I slept in the car somewhere in the neighborhood.

Thursday, August 12, 1971

This morning I slept a bit late. The car had trouble starting again, but I finally managed to get it going. I drove back toward London more or less the same way I had come, but I inevitably got lost. I had intended to go to Ruislip or Rickmansworth, but got fouled up and wound up in Northwood Hills, which is somewhere in between. I found a spot to park near the London Underground station. At the first opportunity, I called American Express from there, but no cable with money had arrived.

I took the subway to the Victoria and Albert Museum, where I spent the entire day looking at British and Asian art, sculpture, costume, metalwork, and furniture. I vaguely remember seeing the Great Bed of Ware, the largest bed in the world. I bought a book in their gift shop.

At 4:30 p.m., I called American Express again, but still nothing from my father. I took the underground back to Northwood Hills and read until dark, then slept in the car.

Friday, August 13, 1971

At 7:00 a.m. I woke up and read for three hours. I got the car started with only minor difficulty, drove to a pay phone, called up the American Express office, and ascertained that the money from my father had arrived. So I parked the car securely and rushed down to Haymarket on the subway to pick it up.

There were two letters waiting for me—one from Dad and one from my friend Anya, who told me where she would be staying in London and when she would be there. I got my Dad's $200 check converted to traveler's checks at the American Express, which cost me $3.

I decided to have one last meal in London before I headed north, so I went to the Casa Mario nearby and had shrimp with mushrooms in wine sauce and some white wine. It was a bit expensive but quite good. I took the subway back to Northwood Hills, got the car going, and wasted a bunch of time trying to find the M1 Motorway that would take me north. I made it 6 miles to Watford and got some gas. There I found a road leading to the M1, but I got into a traffic jam due to incompetent traffic engineering, as well as rampant construction. At this time, the southern extensions of the M1 south from Watford to London were still incomplete, so this may have been part of the problem. Then I lost the M1 and wound up in Hemel Hempstead, where I eventually ran into another northbound entrance.

On the M1 ramp I picked up an American hitchhiker named Ron who was going to Glasgow. (He looked like a guy I knew in Columbus named Bob Di Bella.) He wanted to find work at rock festivals and had been in the UK for four months. I said I was heading to Scotland, so I could take him all the way to Glasgow. At Rugby we exited onto the M6 Motorway and drove through Birmingham, wasting a lot of time in some town along the way where traffic was congested. By then it was raining hard.

We made it to Preston, Lancashire, around 9:00 p.m.—a total of about 200 miles since I had picked up Ron—and we began thinking about a place to stay for the night. We asked a little old lady at a bed and breakfast where there might be an inexpensive place to stay with a shower. She steered us toward downtown

Preston. We found the Cambridge Hotel and its proprietress Mrs. Holacz, who was very nice. I took a room for £1.50, while Ron slept in the car. I had a fantastic bath and slept in what seemed to me a luxurious bed.

Saturday, August 14, 1971

At 7:30 a.m. I woke up and went downstairs for an English breakfast of egg, tomato, sausage, quasi-bacon, corn flakes, bread, toast, jam, marmalade, and coffee. I drove north with Ron on the M6 about 40 miles to Kendal, Cumbria, where we could see some of the beautiful moor-covered hills of the Lake District.

At the Scottish border near Gretna we got stuck in a terrible traffic jam that somehow did some damage to my car's muffler. We bought some food in a market in Ecclefechan, the small town where essayist Thomas Carlyle was born. The muffler was getting very loud, but we drove on to Glasgow, arriving there at 2:30 p.m.

We could not find a youth hostel, and the YMCA was filled up, so we decided to drive through town to the Glasgow Central train station to cash traveler's checks. I parked the car by the River Clyde on Clyde Street, leaving Ron to guard it, and went in search of a financial services office. The banks weren't open on Saturday, and I could not find a travel agency.

When I got back to the car, Ron was having an interaction with a fellow who called himself "James Malcolm." As I recall, the man was a dubious-looking slummy type who had offered to advise Ron on a place to stay if Ron paid him 90p. Ron was suckered in, and Malcolm told him about the Marine House on McAlpine Street. It was only a couple blocks away, so we walked there and found the place, after first eating some of our Ecclefechan market food in a quiet park along the River Clyde.

We decided that we could stay at the Marine House (even though it was pretty sleazy and what the locals called a "flop house") until Monday when I could get some traveler's checks cashed and have someone take a look at the car's muffler.

Ron and I walked around downtown and looked at the Gallery of Modern Art from the outside because it had closed at

5:00 p.m. An equestrian statue of the Duke of Wellington stands in front of the museum, guarding it perhaps. This was long before the Glasgow tradition began in the 1990s of putting a traffic cone on Wellington's head as a light-hearted rebuke to his authority.

In Glasgow Green, a large park along the river, we saw a rock inscribed with "Near this spot in 1765 James Watt conceived the idea for the separate condenser for the steam engine. Patented 1769."

We drove to the edge of town and stopped at a couple petrol stations to ask about prices for a muffler replacement. One place gave us directions to a garage in the city. Someone else volunteered that he knew of a hostel in Balloch by Loch Lomond, as well as a scrap shop, and he said to follow him because he was going there right now.

We followed him 12 miles or so to Balloch, where we discovered that the muffler noise was caused by the exhaust pipe having broken in half and was dragging on the ground. We fixed it temporarily with a rope. Then we drove to the hostel, which was a castle-like building near Duck Bay on Loch Lomond called Auchendennan Lodge. It was a fantastic place with a spiral staircase, towers, a beautiful view, and a low wall all around it. They charged us 5p to park the car and we paid to stay two nights.

Ron and I decided to walk back into Balloch to find a pub. It was quite a bit of a walk (over 2 miles), but pleasant. It had been raining, but conveniently it had stopped. We found a pub with a place to sit down and had a round of stout, then I ordered a screwdriver, but the pub tender did not know how to make one. Ron and I discussed English literature, UFOs, revolution in America, and the benefits of getting up early. However, Ron seemed apathetic on most subjects. On the walk back, I talked about mysticism and the Oneness of Allness that you might experience on an LSD trip. It seemed to interest Ron slightly, but not much.

We got back to the lodge at 10:55 p.m., but it had closed at 10:45. The proprietors were very nasty about our being late and harassed us about it, but they let us in anyway.

Sunday, August 15, 1971

At 7:00 a.m. I woke up and read in bed for a while, then I got up, cleaned out the car, and explored the grounds a bit. Everyone else in the hostel woke up around 8:45 for breakfast and tea. I got Ron together to go for a drive around the loch.

I had some difficulty starting the car again. We picked up two American girls hitchhiking along the A811 with all sorts of luggage and a guitar—the traditional accessory to bring along if you are an American in Europe. They were going to Edinburgh to catch a train for the Isle of Skye on the northwest coast. I don't know what happened to them, as we couldn't take them very far.

Ron and I decided to park in Balloch and walk around a bit to look at the scenery. We crossed over innumerable fences and cow and sheep pastures. It was a beautiful day with a wonderful view of Loch Lomond. We walked a short way to a small promontory on the east side of the loch and rested for awhile. We walked back across the moors and past Mount Misery (Knockour Hill), a minor peak. We walked through many wooded hills and glens and back into Balloch, where we snacked at a café and rested for a while, listening to music on a juke box.

Then we decided to drive up to the hills on the western side of the loch and have a climb. We drove on the A82 past the lodge to a parking place, left the car, and scrambled up a large hill. We fought our way through vast patches of bracken and thorns. Many sheep looked at us with puzzled expressions. There were beautiful burns with refreshing water running down from the hills.

We had an excellent view of Loch Lomond and its islands, but after a while we were getting tired. We rested near the top of the hill next to a bubbling burn, then made our way down in about five minutes along the path it had taken us 90 minutes to ascend. We drove back to the hostel-lodge at 6:00 p.m. or so.

After eating a meal of left-over groceries, I read and drowsed and wrote letters for the rest of the evening. Ron listened to some hostel guests who were singing and playing guitar.

Monday, August 16, 1971

At 7:30 a.m. I got up and awakened Ron. We checked out early and did a quick clean-up of the car. I cranked up the old Austin and we noisily drove off to Balloch. We discovered that the banks there did not open until 9:30 a.m.

We ran across a petrol station and asked them if they knew where the scrap shop we had heard about was. They told us how to find Kennedy's Scrap Shop. We had a small breakfast in Loch Lomond Park, then bought more food in a grocery store and mailed some letters at the post office. Finally, 9:30 rolled around, so we went to a bank and cashed some traveler's checks after waiting a long time.

We rushed over to where we were told that Kennedy's Scrap Shop was, but Mr. Kennedy did not have an exhaust pipe that fit the car, so he directed us over to another scrap shop down the road. This shop did have an A35 exhaust system, and the nice man said he'd put it on and have it ready within an hour.

In the meantime, Ron and I walked around town and visited an old churchyard cemetery. The oldest grave was from the 1740s. Then we had coffee and tea at a small café until 11:15 a.m. The place had all sorts of detective and romance magazines for sale. We hiked back to the scrap shop, but they were still working on the car. The total cost turned out to be £2.50, an excellent price. A garage would have charged three times as much.

We drove away with the engine purring like a kitten. Now it was time to head to the 24-mile-long, one-mile-wide Loch Ness to try to get a glimpse of the monster. Yay!

People have been reporting large animals in Loch Ness since at least 1933. Many witnesses say that when they saw the monster, it could not possibly have been anything else but a large animal. It usually is seen as a long-necked creature with a hump, or as a rounded object like an overturned boat, or as several humps in a line. Its length has been estimated anywhere from 10 to 45 feet. The head is small and flat with two horn-like protrusions on top. Infrequent sightings of the animal on land suggest that it has four short, thick flippers.

Skeptics argue that witnesses are seeing a boat wake, an errant gray seal, a swimming red deer, a wading cow, ducks or geese swimming in tight formation, a sturgeon, an out-of-place basking shark, a mirage, floating trees upended in the water, a vegetation mat, or odd waves.

Cryptozoologists variously hypothesize that Nessie might be a surviving plesiosaur, a surviving archaic whale, an unknown species of large otter, an unknown species of long-necked giant seal, an unknown form of giant amphibian, or even a giant sea slug. No one can know for certain until a specimen is obtained or a reliable sample of DNA can be extracted.

I wanted to visit Loch Ness and see for myself. Ron was having fun, so he decided to stick with me for a while. We picked up two Scottish hitchhikers who were going to the Western Isles. They were very friendly types.

I had a scary time driving along the winding two-lane A82 road around lochs and hills and kills and moors toward Glen Orchy. We had lunch at the Loch Bà viewpoint on Rannoch Moor. There was a huge amount of heather. This loch was quite small and filled with dark water colored by peat. I let the hitchhikers off around Loch Linnhe before I turned north to head for Fort Augustus, where we arrived at 4:30 p.m.

We saw the Caledonian Canal locks in Fort Augustus that step down to the lower level of Loch Ness. We stopped in a grocery store and bought some cookies, then went looking around tourist shops for information and books on Loch Ness but found nothing. After a while we visited a small café in Fort Augustus and had some tea. We walked back to the grocery store and bought more food, postcards, and got a free poster. We drove north looking for a place where Ron and I could rent a boat, but we found nothing.

By pure accident, we ran across Tim Dinsdale's Loch Ness Investigation Bureau (LNI) camp south of Urquhart Castle and stopped in for a visit. A sign outside the camp said, "Loch Ness Investigation Research Headquarters, Visitors Welcome." The camp consisted of an exhibit hut and giftshop, a long wooden shack, two trailers, three cars, and two camper trucks perched 200 feet above the loch, offering an exquisite view for LNI's tripod-mounted 35mm movie camera (with 36-inch telephoto lens) poised outside the shack next to a spinning wind meter.

Tim Dinsdale was a former aeronautical engineer who became fascinated with Nessie and began keeping watch around the loch in April 1960, hoping for a chance to see the beast. On April 23, from a position above Foyers Bay, he spotted with his binoculars a large moving object that seemed unusual because it was not leaving a wake typical of a boat. Using a small Bolex camera, Dinsdale filmed the head and neck of the creature for 60 seconds moving in a zig-zag pattern and leaving a distinctive V wake about 1,300 yards away. About to run out of film, Dinsdale stopped the camera and ran to a closer position, but the animal had disappeared. He returned to the same spot an hour later and used the remaining footage to film a boat crossing the loch for comparison.

In 1966, the Royal Air Force's Joint Air Reconnaissance Intelligence Centre examined Dinsdale's film and confirmed that the object was not a boat and seemed to show an "animate object" 12–16 feet long. A computer enhancement by the Project Urquhart Investigation team in 1993 discovered a shadow behind the animal's head that appears to show a long, sinuous body lying just beneath the surface of the water.

Spurred by this and other Nessie sightings, a Conservative Member of Parliament, David James, established in 1962 the Loch Ness Phenomena Investigation Bureau (LNI) with ornithologist Peter Scott and other interested persons. The group set up film cameras at several points around the loch during the summer and had a certain amount of success in its first two years. Dinsdale directed LNI's surface watch in 1970 and actually lived on-site in 1971 when we visited.

I knew much of this history at the time because of my interest in cryptozoology, which includes lake monsters and sea serpents. (I had actually done a high school science fair project on the history of sea monster sightings.) So I filled in Ron as best I could about Dinsdale and Nessie, then we paid 10p each to get into their exhibit area and giftshop (a shack, really).

I bought Dinsdale's 1966 book on lake monsters, *The Leviathans,* some newsletters, and postcards. I browsed around looking at photos of Nessie, some maps color-coded for the locations of sightings and photographs, the RAF analysis of the Dinsdale film printed out along the wall, and an Identikit rendering of what Nessie might look like.

Then we drove south to look for a place to sleep. At long last, I found a little parking spot near Invermoriston. I had some dinner and gazed at Loch Ness. After a while, I met a Canadian fellow named John, an LNI volunteer who had built a campfire nearby. We talked about the Highlands and British cars and our recent experiences—his were the Reading Rock Festival, an auto accident, and a new job he was getting. He mentioned a nice bookstore in Edinburgh on Leith Street that I should visit. We jabbered on into the night and then I got my sleeping bag out and crashed. I think Ron slept in the car. It was cold.

Tuesday, August 17, 1971

This morning I woke up with midges (small flies) eating me. I had some trouble cranking up the Austin. At 8:00 a.m., I drove back to LNI and talked to a volunteer named Rip Hepple about signing up for LNI's Monster Watch, perhaps just for one day. Rip told me to talk to Tim Dinsdale, who was out on camera watch at the moment.

Tim came back with a volunteer named Graham Snape about 10 minutes later. (I found out two years later, courtesy of the *Flying Saucer Review* magazine, that Snape had seen a white luminous UFO with a purple ring around it flying down the loch only four days earlier.) Tim told me they don't usually take people on for less than one week, but he said they were unusually understaffed at the time and that interest in Nessie is what counts.

Tim showed me how to use the 35mm movie camera at LNI headquarters ("six steps, with a sight-switch"). Dinsdale was a remarkably charming character with a serious attitude and an infectious intensity. Then I met a young Nicholas Witchell, who later wrote a book on Nessie and got a cushy job with the BBC as a reporter. Nick was on watch at the camera positioned adjacent to the headquarters.

I told Ron that I would be staying on at LNI for a day and that he could go into Drumnadrochit and wait if he wanted to. I met all sorts of other people who were volunteering there—Mary, Angela, Holly Arnold, John, Jim, Patty, Angus Dinsdale (Tim's son), the famous author Ted Holiday, Jeff, Wendy, and Murray. I watched the loch all day with the camera. We were supposed to record in a notebook anything that disturbed the surface of the water—even birds or boats. The weather began to get very nice around noon. Tourists came around and asked questions. There were many small fishing boats and cruise boats on the loch, as well as larger ships coming through the Caledonian Canal.

Tim invited me to lunch with all the other volunteers. We talked about the cryptozoologist Ivan T. Sanderson (whose 1961 book *Abominable Snowmen: Legend Come to Life* had first piqued my interest in the topic and who I would later meet in December 1971 at his home in New Jersey) and what a strange fellow he was—especially his experience with the Minnesota Iceman, which turned out to be a complete hoax. Ted Holiday had a clipping from (I think) the *Inverness Courier* about the Florida Skunk Ape that was terrorizing people in the southern swamps. I told Tim I'd like to stay around until Sunday.

Later I found a note on my car from Ron, who said that he had decided to hitchhike to Inverness, and thanks for the ride.

A Swiss scientist named Nageley came by today who was trying to zap the monster with infrared rays—it's supposed to make Nessie confused and bring it to the surface. It hasn't worked yet, but you never know.

There was more boat activity on my watch in the afternoon and more tourists. Patty came around and bothered me all afternoon. I told Holly Arnold (the LNI secretary) that I wanted to become a member of the group and she said she would sign me up. It was flat calm water this afternoon.

A fellow came around with a monster sighting from the Kyle of Tongue, a shallow sea loch on the north coast of Scotland. He saw a head and neck swimming, but he could not take a photo.

We had a dinner of rice and beef around 7:00 p.m. Dinsdale, Murray, Rip Hepple, and the Swiss scientist had all gone down to Urquhart Bay to play with the infrared equipment. They returned around 8:15 and had dinner.

Tim played a tape recording of an interview with someone named Connell, a fellow from Drumnadrochit, who said he had seen Nessie in September 1969—a triple sighting, with three sets of two humps each, swimming along in Urquhart Bay. The loch waters at the time were flat calm. The creatures were about 40 feet long, and their humps were making a peculiar undulating motion.

Tim also showed me photos taken in 1970 with a one-man submarine that released some kind of sex hormones into the water to attract the creatures. It also had sonar equipment.

I played a card game (she called it "spit and switch") with Tim's youngest daughter until 11:00 p.m. I saw the new dinghy that LNI had just acquired, then went to sleep in the "Black Hole" trailer and talked to Jim about his experiences in the US Air Force.

Wednesday, August 18, 1971

At 7:00 a.m. I got up and had a quick coffee and some bread before going on camera watch at Strone, on Urquhart Bay. Tim was up and ready to go. Nick and Mary drove me out to Strone, and Tim familiarized me with this other camera. I had a box of food to eat, but I had to borrow matches from Freddy to light the gas burner.

I saw nothing on the loch except boats. A German couple came and chatted with me for a while. No monster. Mary came and relieved me and Graham came and picked me up to go back to HQ, where I worked public relations for a while in the gift shop. Then I took a watch on the main camera at HQ. I officially joined LNI as a member and paid Wendy my £2.50 dues.

Dinner was at 7:00 p.m. or so. I had planned to walk down to the Lodge pub in Drumnadrochit, which is where the volunteers usually wound up at the end of the day, but the loch was so calm that it enticed me to keep looking at it. Then Holly started playing some music tapes by a girl named Carol—beautiful folk guitar— and then John wanted to stay and play chess with me and he won. Nick Witchell came in with his girlfriend Mary.

Thursday, August 19, 1971

I did not have an assignment this morning, so I slept until 8:30 a.m. then had breakfast with the crew. I hung around the main camera at HQ with Angela, who was on watch. Later on, I drove into Drumnadrochit to mail some postcards.

In the afternoon I went on watch with the camera at Dores Point until 5:30 p.m., but it was boring. Again, no monster. When I was done, I picked up Angela at Strone and we drove back to HQ for dinner. Then I went with Jim and Angela to take a shower at a caravan stop. We came back and went to the Lodge pub in Drumnadrochit for some beers and a dart game, then went to bed.

Friday, August 20, 1971

Today I went on early watch on the camera at Foyers. There were many nosy tourists. I stayed until 1:30 p.m. when I was relieved by John and Dawn. I came back to HQ and did public relations at the exhibit shack. I was finally relieved by Nick, but I had to go help Angela at Invermoriston, so I drove the LNI truck out there. There was some kind of mix-up.

We had dinner, and Pete and Rod came in for a visit from Loch Morar, where there was another group looking for the lake monster there, nicknamed "Morag." I left to carouse at the Lodge in Drumnadrochit. We sang satiric songs on the way back. I didn't get to bed until midnight or so.

Saturday, August 21, 1971

Surprisingly enough, I got up at 6:30 a.m. and went on watch. I talked with Pete most of the day, which turned out to be misty and hazy. Nothing remarkable was seen. I bought a copy of Pete's Loch Morar monster survey. Breakfast and lunch were available in the HQ kitchen. It was a very slow day, and nothing happened. No watches were kept, because the new crew coming on board did not yet know how to operate the cameras. In fact, not all of the new crew had arrived yet. I said goodbye to John and Jim and Nick and Mary, whose volunteer time was up. Angela left a bit later on.

I worked PR for a while in the exhibit shack. After dinner, I read all evening while the others went to the Lodge. I felt somewhat lethargic. I met Janet from Cleveland, Ohio, and I talked to Bill, who was from Salisbury, about the recent Warminster UFO sightings. He said that the older residents scoffed, but the newer people were intrigued. I had to sleep in the kitchen tonight because a new guy named Jon needed my bunk. I waited a long time while Alix and Rod and another guy tried to keep a conversation going in the kitchen. They finally decided to go to bed, so I could then get to sleep.

Sunday, August 22, 1971

Everyone slept late today. I got up because people started trekking into the kitchen. Rather than make them feel uncomfortable, I arose and had some coffee. Then Tim told me to go on watch until breakfast, which I did. I was hoping that Nessie would come out because it was flat calm. No luck.

I had a free breakfast (actually, I had prepaid for my meals only through Friday, but no one said anything; I was nearly out of cash by now). Today was my day to leave, so I got my belongings together and asked Pete and Graham to give the Austin a push to level ground, where I cranked the beast futilely. Tim came out and said they could push me down the hill where I could start the car in gear—he said it was "standard operating procedure for British automobiles." Everyone came out and gave me a push and the car did start—rather hesitantly, though.

I drove north past Urquhart Castle, then circled around and came back to sign the LNI "personality book" and officially say goodbye to everyone. I drove south to Fort Augustus, then up the B852 road on the east side of the loch toward Foyers. There was a thick mist on top of the hills. I was getting low on gas, so I stopped just outside of Foyers and checked the trunk. I discovered I had left my hiking boots at LNI, but it was too late to get them today.

After parking the car, I walked up to Inverfarigaig, where there was a hill I wanted to climb. Mary and Angus had been up this way on Friday, but it had been too rugged for both of them to get to the top. I found the Forestry Commission exhibit that they had visited and wandered around in the hills. I saw some beautiful feral golden pheasants that had been imported from China.

Near the exhibit I located a forester and asked him how to get to the vitrified fort (Dun Deardail) that I had seen on the map. Some Scottish Iron Age forts have had their stones subjected to intense heat (vitrification), causing them to be partially fused or enveloped in a glassy, enamel-like coating. He said the fort was right at the top of the big hill and I should just cross the burn and bear right until I got to the bottom of a cliff face. After I went around the cliff, it was easy going from then on.

I followed the forester's directions—it was quite slippery with dew and encumbered with nettles that sting you if you even brush them gently. I clambered up a treacherous slope to an area covered with heather. Now the insects started getting nasty, but I made it all the way to the top without further difficulty. At the summit was a grassy knoll marked by a cairn with three sticks, which must be the site of the fort. I found a beer can with some kind of inscription on it. I scouted around for other likely locations, but this was the only possible one. I also saw some birch trees that seemed to be marked with axe cuts.

With little difficulty I made my way back down the hill. I walked to the car and started it mostly without a problem (it got stuck once) and drove down to Fort Augustus to a parking lot next to a gas station. I was almost completely out of gas and had very little cash. I ate in a coffee house (expensive), then read for a while, and sacked out in the car.

Monday, August 23, 1971

I got up and started the car easily. I drove to the bank when it opened at 9:30 a.m., cashed a traveler's check, bought some provisions, then went back to the petrol station for gas. I drove up to LNI to pick up my forgotten hiking boots and (incidentally) some other clothes I had left behind.

As I drove on to Inverness, I noticed the loch was flat calm at Urquhart Bay—ripe for a Nessie sighting. At Inverness I picked up two thumbers going south to Edinburgh. They were not very talkative. I took the long but much faster way to Glasgow along the A9. The scenery was not as rugged along this eastern route, but still it was pretty. I dropped the Edinburgh thumbers off at Kinross, where the A91 road branched off to Glasgow.

I arrived in the Glasgow suburbs around 5:00 p.m. (not a good time for shopping), so I parked in a suburb and prepared to sleep there. But some neighbors were giving me some suspicious looks from their windows. This really annoyed me, as well as the noisy kids passing by with their stupid harassing remarks and noises. It was "almost like America." I finally got to sleep around 10:00 p.m. Some police woke me up at midnight and told me that the neighbors were paranoid and that I'd better find another place to kip. It took me 10 minutes to start the car. The neighbors were paranoid about that too. Then I found another suburb and slept in the car. These neighbors didn't even notice I was there.

Tuesday, August 24, 1971

At 6:30 a.m. I woke up and started the car. I drove into downtown Glasgow before any significant traffic started and found a place to park by the River Clyde close to the one that I had when Ron and I were here 10 days earlier. Glasgow is quite 19th-century looking and industrial. I waited until 8:30 and window-shopped until the stores opened at 9:00. I bought two wool fisherman's sweaters and a pair of Polish desert boots, for a total of £9.

At this point I had decided to follow the path of the protagonist of Andrew Sinclair's novel *Gog,* since he started out in Edinburgh and trekked his way through back roads to London. (See the August 9 entry for more background.) I was certainly in the right spot, I had a car to get me to remote and rural areas, I had the novel with me, and I was eager to see the same sights as Gog did on his journey.

I drove 45 miles or so to Edinburgh and parked, walked to Princes Street, and looked at all the historic buildings. I went to the "Writer to a Nation" exhibit on Sir Walter Scott at Waverley Market near the Victorian Gothic Scott Monument. There were illustrations from his books, portraits of his characters, and recordings of readings of his poetry and novels. In the Waverley Room was a suit of armor, a fancy crown on a chair, sound effects, and medieval flags in a tribute to *Ivanhoe*. It was a good show.

I walked a short way east on Princes Street to Leith Street and found the Thistle Inn (it is now the Newsroom Bar and Eatery), which was the first stop on Gog's journey (Chapter I). I went in and had a pint of Younger's Tartan Special. It was a very colorful and lively pub. I walked a mile and a half to Duke Street in Leith without finding the antiquarian bookstore John had told me about. I walked all the way back and discovered it right across the street from the Thistle Inn. (John had told me he "walked a long way" to find it.) I bought two classic books, *An Adventure* by Charlotte Anne Moberly and Eleanor Jourdain (1911) and the two-volume *Isis Unveiled* by Helena Petrovna Blavatsky (1877).

I went back down Princes Street to the car and admired Edinburgh Castle from a distance. I got the car started and drove south on South Bridge Road and South Clark Street to the A701 and passed the University of Edinburgh. I found the Liberton Cemetery near Liberton Brae and emerged on Burdiehouse Road at the edge of the city and followed it to the roundabout where Gog meets Merlin Blake Smith (Chapter I).

I took back roads over the North Esk and South Esk River for about 12 miles and found the entrance to the "great tall-windowed" Arniston House near the village of Temple (Chapter IV). From here I took the B7007 over the Moorfoot Hills ("wallowing like stranded whales, encrusted by the barnacled lines of the stone walls and by occasional patches of weedy spruce") toward Innerleithen. It's a really beautiful drive—you don't get to see this on the motorways. I saw the town coat of arms with St. Ronan and passed the old Innerleithen churchyard mentioned in the book (Chapter VI), although it was closed. Just to the south, I drove past the historic Traquair House ("standing among its trees in tall granite and freestone rubble, with its windows slit against arrows and crows") without stopping, as it was starting to get late. I parked at a rest area along the B709 road with Glengaber Hill on one side and Deuchar Burn ("full of booby-traps of bottomless bog") adjacent on the other side (Chapter VI). I filled some water bottles, ate supper, and slept in the car.

Wednesday, August 25, 1971

At 7:30 a.m. I woke up to a sheep drive along a nearby moor. Intrigued, I took a short hike over the moor, but there was nothing to see except a view of rolling hills and a bunch of sheep. When I returned, I had serious problems starting the car. I hand-cranked for 45 minutes with no result. In desperation, I flagged some cars down and the drivers gave me a push so I could get a running start.

The Austin sputtered all the way back to Innerleithen. I turned it around to go back south, but the car stalled, and I could not start it because I had left the crank back at the rest area on the B709 near the moor. I walked almost all the way back to pick it up, but at last I got a ride from a friendly Scottish farmer. The car started on the first crank.

In Innerleithen I drove around and located a garage, the car sputtering all the way. The mechanic, who was wearing a brown suit coat, said that I needed a new radiator hose, but he didn't have one, so he directed me to a nearby scrap shop. The scrap man was quite friendly. He did have a hose and only charged me 70p to install it. The car sputtered no longer.

Gog walked south on the moors, but I had to stay on the roads, so I drove through Selkirk and across Ettrick Water to Hawick (pronounced "hoik") in the Scottish Borders, where I got gas and provisions. I found the movie theater mentioned in the book (Chapter VI).

Borthwick Water was a bit out of the way, and I concluded, based on the book's reference to mill traffic, that its reference to an overpass at Borthwick actually was meant to signify the bridge over the River Teviot in Hawick (Chapter VII). Then I drove further south on the B6399 to visit the haunted Hermitage Castle (Chapter VIII). Built around 1240, the castle's square, block-like, unturreted look makes it one of the most atmospheric fortresses in Scotland.

Hermitage Castle has many ghosts, but its most famous wraith is Mary, Queen of Scots, who supposedly can be seen here walking hand in hand with her third husband, James Hepburn, the 4th Earl of Bothwell, who held the castle. After the birth in 1566 of her only son, the future King James I of England, to Lord Darnley, Mary supposedly rode her horse 50 miles in one day from Jedburgh to the Hermitage when she heard Bothwell had been wounded. They married the following year after Darnley was murdered, even though Bothwell was implicated (but acquitted) of the crime.

The creepiest ghost by far at Hermitage Castle is that of William II de Soules (aka Lord Soulis), a Scottish Border noble during the Wars of Scottish Independence. In 1320, he was convicted of treason against King Robert the Bruce, imprisoned in Dumbarton Castle, and died the following year under mysterious circumstances.

Legend has it that Lord Soulis was involved in black magic and had a familiar spirit named Robin Redcap, with whom he made a devilish deal. In return for unlimited wealth and power, he abducted village children, brought them to the castle, and slaughtered them mercilessly. When the villagers found out and were confronted with the corpses inside the castle, they imprisoned Soulis, prepared a vat of molten lead at the Ninestane Rig, a megalithic stone circle near the castle, and lowered him into it, boiling him alive. He allegedly haunts the Hermitage, calling out to children to come and play with his special friend, Robin Redcap.

Of course, the story does not fit in with the historical record, so some suspect the legend refers to Ranulf de Soules, who was murdered by his servants in 1208.

Another legend about Lord Soulis is that he defeated a Northumbrian giant, the Cout o' Kielder, who wore a suit of armor that was impervious to all weapons. Soulis tricked him and knocked him into a river, where he drowned from the weight of his armor. The site is today known as the Drowning Pool and a large burial mound is said to be the Cout's grave.

I took a tour of the castle and found the giant Cout o' Kielder's grave site and the Hermitage's drowning pool. I talked to the castle manager, who told me that the Ninestane Rig was two miles northeast of the castle. He described the history of Lord Soulis and told me how to get to the Bloody Bush toll pillar (a marker on the border between Scotland and England that was about a 4-mile walk, but a 45-minute drive) and about the notorious terrier dogs (phantoms, perhaps? I don't recall what he was talking about) and how lucky I was to visit today because he knew all about this stuff.

It was time for a picnic, so I retrieved some food from the car and sat down on the castle grounds. I found a single-track forestry road (B6357) near Liddel Water that went to Bloody Bush via Larriston Fells. I made it all the way to about three-quarters of a mile from the site when I noticed the Austin appeared to be leaking water. Rather than get stuck in the middle of nowhere, I sped south to a garage in the village of Newcastleton, where I found a mechanic who said it was my overflow pipe, and he adjusted it.

I drove to Kielder, across the border in England, via the picturesque Saughtree Road. I fortuitously stopped at a post office on the way to Kielder Castle, where I visited the Forestry Commission. They told me I could almost get to Bloody Bush via forestry roads, but I would have to walk part of the way. I drove and drove and walked and walked. The sun was getting low. I did find the woodsman's hut where Gog and Cluckitt slept (Chapter VIII), but not the Bloody Bush toll marker.

Then I drove back along the River North Tyne southeast to the village of Falstone and found the Blackcock Inn ("a pub lined with painted dark wood and low plaster ceilings," Chapter IX). I did not go inside; instead, I drove down the road past the Chirdon Burn to Bellingham. I found a spot by the side of the road to kip and kipped.

Thursday, August 26, 1971

This morning I woke up worried that I might have trouble starting the car, but I had relatively little difficulty. I drove south from Bellingham through Wark to Simonburn, where I stopped at a grocer's to ask directions. I bought a pint of dark ale.

I drove to a spot where my map showed a Roman camp by Hadrian's Wall, possibly Black Carts Turret, a small fort along the wall, which was a defensive structure running 73 miles across England that was begun in 122 CE by the Roman Emperor Hadrian. It was intended to deter raids into Roman Britain by the Pictish peoples of Caledonia living to the north. I feasted on some breakfast by the wall. Part of the structure in this spot had opened up a bit, exposing huge stones with grooves cut into them. There was a ditch on both sides. I found an old piece of very brittle copper and fantasized that it might have been left by a Roman soldier. Then I wandered around and located a hawthorn tree that might have been the one where Gog slept (Chapter IX).

Next I drove down the road to Chesters Roman Fort and Museum (Chapter XI), less than two miles down the B6138, and paid the admission price to see it. Known to the Romans as Cilurnum, this cavalry station near the River Tyne near Walwick, Northumberland, had bathhouses, military headquarters, barracks, latrines, and gates. The site guarded a bridge, Chesters Bridge, carrying a Roman road across the Tyne. Massive abutments of this bridge survive across the river from the fort, which housed some 500 cavalrymen and was occupied until the Romans left Britain in the 5th century.

Pioneering excavations in the 19th century yielded one of the best collections of inscriptions and sculpture along the wall. By the time Roman rule in England ended in 410 CE, the fort at Chesters had dwindled in size and had been cut off from central authority for several decades. It is uncertain whether the last garrison was removed to serve elsewhere, or whether they were left to fend for themselves. The museum displayed many artifacts—coins, pediments, inscriptions, statues, tools, a leather shoe, a jawbone, lots of pottery.

I drove about two miles down the road to the Battle of Heavenfield site by St. Oswald's Church along Hadrian's Wall southeast of Chollerford (Chapter XI). This is where the Christian King Oswald of Northumbria defeated a Welsh army in 634 CE and set up a cross. A wooden replica stands there today.

Then I went about six miles further to Corbridge (Chapter XII), with its "tall old grey houses," where I mailed a postcard and bought some food in a market. I stopped for a bit by the River Tyne to have a snack.

I passed through Whittonstall, another 9 miles to the southeast, where there is a restaurant and lodging house called the Anchor Inn. Then I drove past the industrial town of Consett and the bungalows of Leadgate through the Grey Country all the way to Durham (Chapter XIII), which I reached at 2:30 p.m. I left the car in a parking lot and walked down North Road through the old railroad overpass and saw the 1875 Durham Miners' Hall, now the Essoldo Cinema (which closed shortly after I was there and in 2023 houses the Loft Durham nightclub and J. M. Foley's Irish Pub) and walked over the River Wear bridge to Durham Castle and Durham Cathedral.

The cathedral is incomparably imposing, with its relics of St. Cuthbert and Venerable Bede, and its exquisite 12th-century Romanesque architecture and medieval paintings. I wandered through it, noting the V-shaped designs on the columns in its nave. Some say that Durham Cathedral is one of the most impressive churches in Europe, and I would have to agree. Sir Walter Scott described the dual cathedral-castle in this fashion: "Grey towers of Durham / Yet well I love thy mixed and massive piles / Half church of God, half castle 'gainst the Scot."

The 11th-century Durham Castle adjacent to the cathedral is now part of the university, thus there was a fee to go inside for a guided tour, which I declined. As I was walking outside, a Britisher asked me where the university was; I told him that Durham Castle was part of it. He mentioned that he had visited many cathedrals before, but Durham was the only city he knew that did not openly celebrate the cathedral smack in its center. I replied that maybe this was because the city looks so 19th century, while its cathedral is still in the 11th century.

I then went back to the car and drove 45 miles south to Borrowby, North Yorkshire (Chapter XV), arriving around 5:45 p.m. I had a light supper in town, then drove to a car park on the A19 south of town. Read and slept. I need to cash traveler's checks tomorrow and change Scottish pounds to English pounds.

Friday, August 27, 1971

The car started nicely. I waited until about 9:00 a.m. before I went looking for a bank, because they usually don't open until 9:30. A police cruiser came through the car park once but didn't give me any trouble. I drove to the Borrowby post office, but the clerk said there were no banks in town, and I would have to go to either Northallerton or Thirsk.

I obtained some gas, then drove 5 miles south to Thirsk and waited until 9:30 when the Nationwide Bank opened. They had no currency exchange rate, so after waiting unproductively a while, I went to Lloyd's and got a traveler's check cashed. My money is getting quite low.

My next destination is the Yorkshire moors. I proceeded on back roads over the Hambleton Hills ("their limestone and grit scarps as spume on top of the choppy swell of the foothills") and past Boltby Moor and the town of Boltby, then through Old Byland—a pleasant, rolling, pastoral landscape.

Then I came to Ryedale and visited Rievaulx Abbey along the River Rye (Chapter XV). I paid 2½p to park the car and 7½p to get inside the grounds. The Gothic abbey has been in ruins since the dissolution of the monasteries in 1538, with no roof and much grass growing in the aisles. It is both a peaceful and impressive site, and it was fun to see the arches, flying buttresses, cloister, and abbot's quarters.

Afterward I drove across the high parkland of Scawton Moor to Byland Abbey (Chapter XVII), which didn't seem like it was open, but I could see a few people walking around inside. Byland is even more ruined than Rievaulx, with only one arched wall and part of a tower remaining. I didn't particularly feel like paying to get in when there was such a good view from the road, so I just admired it from a distance.

Next I drove through the village of Coxwold and sped directly toward York. As I approached, I could see Rowntree's cocoa factory in the distance. Then I parked on a side street and walked toward York Minster (Chapter XVIII), the city's massive cathedral. First, I looked around the old town center for The Pick and the Mattock pub, but it either no longer existed or it was a literary invention in the *Gog* book. There were all sorts of fascinating little shops on centuries-old narrow streets, as well as antiquarian bookstores and old churches and old houses.

York Minster was being renovated, with much construction materials and scaffolding all around. Its foundations were also getting bolstered. The window called the Five Sisters, the largest medieval stained-glass window in the British Isles, is set in the north transept. Each segment is 53 feet high, and all five contain more than 100,000 pieces of glass.

Outside, I walked down a narrow medieval street called The Shambles with many ancient timber-framed residences jutting out above the storefronts below, supported by black beams of wood, many of them "aslant and agley with warping and subsidence." Then I went inside an old church, St. Michael Le Belfrey, that had on display a photostatic copy of Guy Fawkes's baptismal registration. This was indeed the very church where the gunpowder plotter had been baptized in 1570.

And now it's off to Wales! I went back to the car and had a bit of trouble finding the correct road out of town. I drove through Harrogate and hopped on a motorway into Wales, the stronghold of the Silures and the Ordovices and other Celtic tribes. The land has beautiful castles (such as Penrhyn), mountains, forests, a rugged coast, and medieval fortifications.

I began looking for a bed and breakfast because I was getting tired and needed a bath. I found a B&B near St. Asaph, Denbighshire, called Pant Ifan—perhaps it was the current Pant Ifan Goch, on Holywell Road, although it must have been fixed up considerably since then. In 1971, it was an old farmhouse and barn with cattle and chickens. The proprietress was very welcoming. For £1.25, she let me have the room of someone who had left for a few days. On the wall of the room was a thermometer in the shape of a key, with the inscription: "Come to Columbus, Ohio, and discover America. The City Beautiful, M. E. Sensenbrenner, Mayor. Home of the Buckeyes." Maynard Sensenbrenner was mayor of Columbus in 1954–1960 and 1964–1972, so he was still serving when I visited this small place in Wales. Columbus is just something you can't get away from. It follows you wherever you go, even in small farmhouses in Wales.

I slept a wondrous sleep after taking an exquisite bath.

Saturday, August 28, 1971

At 8:45 a.m., I had breakfast with an American family from New York who were staying at the farmhouse. They had also just returned from the Scottish Highlands but were only spending two weeks in Britain. I asked the proprietress where she had gotten that thermometer, and she said her husband had been in Columbus one year for the Ohio State Fair to view some farm equipment (or else exhibit it).

The car started easily enough today. I drove about 34 miles to Bangor and picked up a British couple who were hitchhiking to Holyhead on Holy Island, Anglesey, which is where I was headed (Chapter XIX). The island is called "holy" because there are many stone circles and other megalithic burial chambers scattered about. The two Brits were in the process of emigrating to Ireland, which was supposed to have a better quality of life than England— slower, with less hassles. A lot of hippie types are doing this, the man said. He gave me the address of a chap named Stringbean in Luton, Bedfordshire, who might want to buy my car. I let them off in Holyhead, where I bought some provisions.

I drove south to Trearddur Bay on the west coast of Holy Island and parked and read and sat outside. Some people were swimming in the very cold water. The weather was cloudy, and it was drizzling off and on. Later, I drove farther south to another beach where I sat out for a while, but it had gotten much colder. I went back inside the car and read. I found a spot by the side of the road where I could park and sleep. I read W. Raymond Drake's 1964 ancient astronaut book, *Gods or Spacemen,* until it got dark.

Sunday, August 29, 1971

It had rained all night and was still raining when I woke up. I stayed in the car and read all morning. It finally started to clear up at 1:00 p.m., so I started the car and drove back to Trearddur Bay. As a matter of fact, it turned into a lovely day, so I left the car at the bay and walked across the island to the east, climbing around in the be-heathered rocks. I walked down a dirt road past an aluminum factory, but I couldn't get to the beach at Penrhos Coastal Park on the east side of the island, because I was blocked by a large area where the factory was dumping waste.

I returned to Trearddur Bay and wandered around the picturesque rocky coves there. It was eerily beautiful, with the waves and the wind and the rocks and the seaweed. I walked a long way around the area, saw many Llwybrau cerdded (public footpath) signs, then returned to the car to find a spot for a picnic along "Albion's ancient Druid rocky shore," as William Blake called it. I found a picturesque area, had some supper, and read some more. Soon it began to get colder, so I climbed into the car again for a while, then drove back to the same spot as last night to sleep.

Monday, August 30, 1971

As soon as I woke up, I got the car started and left, driving across Anglesey through the village of Llanfairpwllgwyngyll, whose even longer Welsh name with 58 characters is said to be the longest place name in Europe. (In English, it translates to "St. Mary's Church in the Hollow of the White Hazel near to the Rapid Whirlpool of Llantysilio of the Red Cave.") I wanted to buy a postcard from there and mail it stamped with its distinctive postmark, but nothing was open at 8:00 a.m.

Somewhere just past Bangor I picked up an 18-year-old German hitchhiker named Johannes. We cruised all the way through Wales, speaking German. Johannes wanted to go to Salisbury, which was indirectly on my route to Devon. We stopped at a café for some coffee and chocolate, talking about science, American and German politics, women, and our experiences in Europe.

We picked up a Welsh hitchhiker who was only going a short way to Hereford. He was very interested in America and apparently did not see many American tourists in his home area. We let him off in Leominster, but just before that he showed us a copy of *Oz* magazine, an underground British and Australian publication that was causing a great deal of controversy because of its supposed obscene content. The British issues are now rare and command high prices among collectors.

Johannes and I began talking about music, and it turned out that he plays violin, guitar, and a couple other instruments in a musical group. He was a big fan of French violinist Jean-Luc Ponty.

We trucked into Stratford-upon-Avon around 3:30 p.m. and found a place to park. We walked around and realized that most of the stores were closed because it was a bank holiday, apparently a common occurrence on Mondays. We found a café with cheaper prices than most (though still a bit pricey), paying 19p for eggs, sausage, and chips.

Then we went to the half-timbered house on Henley Street where William Shakespeare was born in 1563, paid the 15p admission fee in the Shakespeare Centre museum next door, and browsed the exhibits and the Bard's home. Mostly the museum featured restored Elizabethan furniture, antiquarian editions of *Holinshed's Chronicles* and *Plutarch's Lives* (both of which Will used as historical sources), a First Folio (1623), a Second Folio (1632), deeds, Will's will, and a "baby minder" (a rocking cradle). At the time I thought it was kind of a rip-off, but I suspect I would have a different opinion today.

The town seemed to have many places where "Will did this here" or "Will was here." Johannes and I mused that at some point we would run across a sign saying "Will pissed here" and that admission would be 20p (children 10p, dogs and Episcopalians free).

We went to a nicely restored church (probably the Guild Chapel) that had faded medieval paintings. We walked through some Elizabethan gardens and noticed a Bible exhibit but did not visit it.

We found a hostel directory and discovered that there were no youth hostels directly on the route that I was taking to Totnes in Devon. Johannes had to stay in a hostel because he had not brought a sleeping bag. He had difficulty deciding what to do, so I decided for him. There was a hostel in Stratford, and I figured that his best chance for finding another ride was here. I hated to drop him off abruptly like that, but that was the best option. I drove him to the hostel and we cooked a meal there. (He did not tell me before I heated them up that he did not like meat pies.) So I had two meat pies and some tea that I brought.

I said goodbye to Johannes and set off for Devon, driving into the night until about 11:00 p.m., a journey of about 115 miles. I picked up two Irish hitchhikers who accidentally left some bread in the car. They were traveling somewhere to do some plum picking. I got lost in Bristol, but I picked up a thumber who was just going a short way. He showed me the right route to get to Taunton. I slept in a parking spot just outside Taunton.

Tuesday, August 31, 1971

I woke up and breezed past Taunton and Exeter for 55 miles and arrived in the historic market town of Totnes at 9:00 a.m., "the grey town falling down from its tumulus through narrow streets of tall houses to the bends of the River Dart" (Chapter XX).

The locals were all dressed up in quaint costumes to celebrate the Totnes Festival this week. I walked along the colonnaded Butterwalk arcade, a Tudor covered walkway built to protect the dairy products sold there from the elements. I found the tall (120-foot) west tower of the old Devonian sandstone church, which turned out to be St. Mary's Church on High Street. Then I strolled through the East Gate Arch (with a clock on each side) to the Brutus Stone, set into the pavement on Fore Street. The *Gog* book makes the stone a big deal, so I wanted to be sure to see it.

According to the 12th-century Geoffrey of Monmouth's historically unreliable *History of the Kings of Britain,* the legendary Brutus of Troy, a descendant of the Trojan hero Aeneas, allegedly came ashore with Phoenician sailors on the "coast of Totnes," becoming Britain's first king. Later legend has it that he stepped on the boulder that became the Brutus Stone and proclaimed, "Here I stand and here I rest. And this town shall be called Totnes." However, the stone was first mentioned as a marker of this event only in the late 17th century, and it was far from the shoreline, even in antiquity. More likely, the stone was either a boundary marker or the spot where the town crier stood to relay the news.

A few other sites in town sounded intriguing—Totnes Castle on the hill and the 16th-century Totnes Guildhall—but I was feeling some mental pressure to move on. I walked back down Fore Street, across the River Dart at Totnes Bridge, and past the Seymour Hotel (no longer standing in 2023) on Bridgetown Road to the spot where I had parked the car.

Now it's off some 8 miles northeast to Newton Abbot (Chapter XX), past the elegant Pig and Whistle on the A381 near Littlehempston, with its pub sign showing a large piggy blowing a police whistle. Then I located the 1874 graystone Mackrell almshouses (now flats and cottages) in Wolborough Street and the 1904 Passmore Edwards Public Library on Market Street, impressively decorated with yellow terracotta moldings over the windows and doorways.

There was a hellish traffic jam all the way through Newton Abbot. Eighteen miles north in Exeter, I looked for the Duke of Wellington pub (Chapter XXI), but it was apparently fictional. Instead, I went into the atmospheric Turk's Head pub on High Street in Exeter for a half pint of pale ale.

I stopped for a quick visit to Exeter Cathedral with its beatific vaulted ceiling. Adjacent to the 14th-century cathedral were some archaeological excavations for the 7th-century predecessor Church of St. Mary Major, where some Roman and Saxon sites had also been uncovered. Detracting from all this splendor, Exeter seemed to me to smell like overripe limburger cheese.

On the road to Glastonbury, I picked up a 30-ish hitchhiker who was headed to Taunton, Somerset. His car was being fixed and he did not want his wife to know that it needed repairs. He was a construction contractor who thought the US should be fighting in Vietnam, even though he voted a straight Labour ticket—kind of archetypal working class, but a friendly chap. We encountered a massive traffic jam for 45 minutes, then I dropped him off in Taunton before making my way to the abbey ruins.

Glastonbury Abbey (Chapter XXIII) was smack in the middle of town, so I parked and paid the Eintrittsgeld to visit the sacred soil of the monastery and Arthur's Grave and St. Joseph of Arimathea's thorn tree. It was a nice place to visit, but to me it did not feel particularly holy.

From at least the 12th century, Glastonbury has been associated with the legend of King Arthur, a connection promoted by medieval monks who asserted that Glastonbury was the site of the mythical isle of Avalon. Christian legends claim that the abbey was founded by the famed but mysterious Joseph of Arimathea in the 1st century (although it was really established in the early 8th century and became Benedictine in the 10th, lasting until the dissolution of the monasteries in 1539). In 1184, a great fire destroyed most of the buildings, causing pilgrimages to fall off. During reconstruction in 1191, the supposed discovery of King Arthur and Queen Guinevere's tomb in the cemetery provided fresh impetus for pilgrims. A contemporaneous account was given by chronicler Giraldus Cambrensis in his *De principis instructione* (1193), according to which Abbot Henry de Sully had commissioned a search, discovering at the depth of 16 feet a massive hollowed-oak trunk containing two skeletons. Above it, under the covering stone, was a leaden cross with the unmistakably specific inscription *Hic jacet sepultus inclitus rex Arthurus in insula Avalonia* ("Here lies interred the famous King Arthur on the Isle of Avalon"). Historians have dismissed the find, attributing it to a monkish publicity stunt performed to raise funds to repair the abbey. A sign still marks the location of the find, and I bought a postcard of Arthur's Grave to mail to my father.

St. Joseph of Arimathea's thorn tree at Glastonbury is a form of common hawthorn found in the area. Unlike ordinary hawthorns that flower once in the spring, the Glastonbury thorn flowers twice a year, in both winter and spring. According to legend, Joseph visited Glastonbury with the Holy Grail around 60 CE and thrust his staff into Wearyall Hill, which then grew into the original thorn tree. Joseph's presence in Glastonbury remains controversial, but the thorn is first mentioned in a pamphlet published by Richard Pynson in 1520 called *Lyfe of Joseph of Armathie,* which was almost certainly commissioned by the monks of Glastonbury. It was seen as a mark of divine favor, proof that Glastonbury was "the holyest erth of Englande." The thorn kept Glastonbury's legendary history alive during the centuries between the dissolution of the abbey and the town's renaissance as a spiritual center in the 20th century. The tree on the grounds of the abbey was certified dead in June 1991 and cut down the following February. However, many cuttings were taken from it before its destruction.

On my way to Shepton Mallet, I drove past Glastonbury Tor, a large, terraced hill that features the remains of a medieval church (St. Michael's Tower) at its top. The Tor seems to have been called Ynys yr Afalon ("The Isle of Avalon") by the early Britons, underscoring its connection with King Arthur. I looked for, but could not find, the Ponter's Ball Dyke, an earthwork mentioned in the *Gog* book (Chapter XXIII). The site was about three miles east of Glastonbury on the A361 road, but there was no signpost.

Near Shepton Mallet, I found the Cannard's Grave Inn (now called The Highwayman) at Cannard's Grave, named after Giles "Tom" Cannard, a 17th-century publican at the inn who apparently engaged in theft, gambling, forgery, and fencing stolen property. He was hanged after he was caught with 10 stolen sheep in his yard. Legend has it that he was the last man hanged in England for sheep stealing.

Then I drove about 12 miles through the Mendip Hills and on to King Alfred's Tower on Kingsettle Hill, Wiltshire, where I decided to camp out in the nearby woods. This 161-foot-tall triangular tower is an architectural folly completed in 1772 by the banker Henry Hoare II, who intended to commemorate the end of the Seven Years' War with France and the accession of King George III. However, a statue of King Alfred the Great of Wessex stands above the entrance to the tower, his right hand on his heart and his left hand on his sword, and an inscription notes that it was near this spot in 879 CE that the king rallied the Anglo-Saxon army against the Danes prior to the Battle of Edington (or Ethandun) in Wiltshire.

Wednesday, September 1, 1971

The sound of hounds barking and someone shouting, "Good morning, milord," woke me up. I saw a blur of red coats and black hats. It was a fox hunt! The scene was very strange, especially in the context of King Alfred's Tower. However, the surrounding land is part of the privately owned Stourhead estate, and the lord of the manor was undoubtedly in the mood for a run with the hounds. I hope he enjoyed himself, since the practice has been banned in England since 2004.

Somewhere I asked someone where a bank was, and I drove north toward Frome to find it. I parked in a lot for 5p (that was a mistake). I waited around until 9:30 a.m. and mailed a postcard. At the bank I cashed my third-to-last traveler's check, then drove out to the outskirts of town to buy food.

Next I drove back south through Batcombe on the way to the "high meadows and chalky linen" of White Sheet Hill (Chapter XXV), the site of an Iron Age hill fort in Wiltshire. I drove up a gravel road a long way, then got out and walked. A sign told me that the place was used for artillery shelling when a red flag was displayed, but I did not see the sign until I had finished visiting the hill fort. Oops. At least no red flag was out. The White Sheet Camp was nothing much, just some mounds, and certainly not the "causewayed enclosure" promised in the *Gog* book. But I found a nice piece of flint, which I kept and still have. I stumbled upon an ordnance survey triangulation marker.

Then I drove down a couple of miles through Mere and past the Old Ship Inn on Castle Street, then southeast through

Semley to Donhead St. Mary, all of these places fairly close together. Somehow, I managed to find the Old Salisbury Way to Chiselbury Camp (Chapter XXV), another Iron Age hill fort. The road was quite rough and narrow, so I only drove part of the way and walked the rest. The camp was merely a circle of earthworks, below which were some emblems outlined in chalk on a hillside (the Wiltshire Regiment, the YMCA, and others). Some of these were carved into the chalk by soldiers garrisoned near Fovant during the First World War, and today they are called the Fovant Badges. Chalk outcrops were everywhere.

Then I drove 4.5 miles through Compton Chamberlayne to Barford St. Martin. I tried finding the way from Barford to Grim's Ditch (Chapter XXVI) in Grovely Wood (on the Wiltshire and Dorset borders), but there was no road, so I drove to Great Wishford and tried to approach it from the east. I found a back road to Grovely Wood and drove and walked part of the way since I did not want to get the Austin 35 stuck in the arse end of nowhere, as the locals might say. It started to rain. I gave up on finding Grim's Ditch, even though I was in the right area. In any case, the pre-Roman earthwork was said to be "clogged with leaf mould and bracken and brier." I drove off to Salisbury and made a quick visit in the drizzle to the ruin of the Norman castle in Old Sarum (Chapter XXVII)—an area north of town where the earliest settlements of Salisbury are located.

Afterward, I drove out of town on the road north leading to Stonehenge and found a place to park in a layby. A cop stopped by and woke me up briefly early in the morning.

Thursday, September 2, 1971

This morning I decided to wait a bit later than usual to move on, as I might as well relax a bit. When I finally decided to try to start the car around 9:00 a.m., some cops pulled up and gave me a slight hassle. They were friendly, but still a bit annoying. They took my name and registration number. Apparently, a traffic warden had reported that there might be someone "lying dead in that car." They finally left me alone, though, and I got the car started.

I drove through Salisbury again and saw its cathedral from a distance, then I drove on back roads southeast through Whiteparish and Romsey, where I found the Romsey Working Men's Conservative Club, formerly the site of the Old Swan Inn, where in 1642 two soldiers of Oliver Cromwell's army were hanged from a wrought-iron sign bracket on its outside wall (Chapter XXIX).

Then I drove the 20 miles to Winchester, where I found a place to park. I began walking toward the cathedral, but along the way I found a little second-hand bookstore, which I browsed through. I bought a 1933 copy of *Cassell's World Pictorial Gazetteer* for 65p, then walked on to the Cathedral, which is featured in the *Gog* book (Chapter XXIX), and I marveled at its Gothic nave and arches, its Norman transepts, the great 1851 organ, the exquisite stained glass in the Great East Window and the Lady Chapel, and the mortuary chests of former bishops and kings of Wessex.

As I walked back to where the car was parked, I could not get the 1966 song "Winchester Cathedral" by the New Vaudeville Band out of my head. I went into a pub to read and drank some stout. I walked back to the cathedral because my guidebook said King Arthur's Round Table was on display at the Great Hall of Winchester Castle.

Unfortunately, I couldn't find the Great Hall, even though it was only a few minutes' walk from the cathedral, so I wandered around to a drugstore where I purchased one of Judith Merril's science-fiction anthologies. I read it in the car for a while, then decided to drive halfway to Luton, find somewhere to sleep, then proceed to Luton the next day, where I would try to find Stringbean, who the British hitchhikers had told me about, and sell him my car.

I drove up through Buckinghamshire to Ascot and Slough, but I got fouled up looking for an out-of-the-way place to sleep. I followed timber camp signs and wound up going in a circle, but I finally found a place where there weren't so many policemen and read and slept.

Friday, September 3, 1971

In the morning I purchased 2 gallons of gas and drove out to Luton, where I asked people how to get to Stringbean's address. Around noon, I found Stringbean's place on Pirton Road. I saw some people looking at me from a window in Stringbean's flat. I parked the car and walked to the flat, and the people rushed to let me in. It was Maryann and Ollie, who said it seemed to them like I was coming for a visit. They wanted to invite me in for tea. Maryann was deaf in one ear and had a little kid named Simon. I had some tea with them, smoked a joint, and discussed John Goodchild (a British mystic), my adventures, music, social problems, and Loch Ness. They invited me to stay at their place as long as I wanted, because I sounded like I was tired of sleeping in my car. That was indeed the case.

Maryann and Stringbean were going to Cornwall that night on holiday. Stringbean came back from his job of street sweeping around 5:00 p.m., bringing presents for Simon's first birthday today. Ollie cooked an excellent dinner of sausages, eggs and potatoes, and peas. Stringbean said he didn't know anyone offhand who wanted to buy a car, nor did he know anything about a supposed rock festival in Hyde Park on Saturday where Jack Bruce and King Crimson were allegedly playing.

Stringbean was kind of an odd fellow, and "rather dense," according to Ollie. She said he'd been bad off before Maryann cleaned him up and took him in. He was nice, though, and built large (kind of like Gog). He really liked his kid. Ollie had been married too and had a kid as well, but she was divorced. Her kid was on vacation with an aunt somewhere. Ollie and I discussed the occult all evening—appearances of the dead and poltergeists, witchcraft covens, and theories of elementals. Then I said goodnight and slept on the living room couch.

Saturday, September 4, 1971

Ollie slept late, so I did not bother getting up until I decided to make some tea in the kitchen. I took a nice bath, then had some bread and treacle for breakfast. We discussed music and other things. Ollie has a tremendous capacity for talking about almost everything and everybody. I thought briefly about driving to Hyde Park to see if there was going to be a Jack Bruce music concert, but I was kind of getting lazy.

Ollie was calling up her neighbors to see if anyone wanted to buy a car, but there were no takers. I decided I should show some appreciation for Ollie's hospitality, so I took her out to the Kashmir Indian Restaurant in Luton, a Pakistani establishment. There were many Jamaicans and Pakistanis dining there. It was excellent food. I had a sort of curry with lobster and meat, and guava for dessert.

We went to see Ollie's friends Caroline and Mick afterward. Bobby was there too, with a couple of other people who were tripping out. We listened to Crosby, Stills, Nash, and Young's *Four-Way Street* and a couple other English groups. Mick described his "fuzz-baiting escapade," apparently a prank on the local police. They were all friendly countercultural types. We stayed until about 11:00 p.m. or so, then left. We had some tea when we got back. I was quite tired by this time, so I went to sleep quickly.

Sunday, September 5, 1971

I got up and made some tea. I didn't know whether I should leave for London today or not, but there really was no reason to go to the city on a Sunday, so I stayed on. Ollie did not mind.

We had a breakfast of oats and raisins. We sat around and talked all day. Ollie had many stories to tell about people she knew in Luton. I read for a while, and we talked about moon legends before retiring.

Monday, September 6, 1971

It was time to sell my car and find my friend Anya in London, so I left fairly early in the morning, thanking Ollie profusely. I gave her my paperback copy of Andrew Sinclair's *Gog* to read. I drove into London as far as I could (Finsbury Park, I think). Then I walked to the London Underground and made sure that the Parkway Hotel was over by Paddington, so I took the subway to Paddington and wandered around for about 90 minutes until I found it.

The clerk at the desk said there was no Anya staying there, but I should try the Queensway or the Prince Regent Hotel nearby. I searched for the Queensway and found it, but Anya was not in, but now at least I know where she is staying. I walked back along Oxford Street to my car.

By this time it was 4:00 p.m. and I drove back to the Queensway during rush hour. A taxi driver saw me drinking a soda pop and commented (as we were stalled in traffic), "Ye'll need a whole lunch before ye get through wi' this traffic." I parked in front of the Queensway and waited for Anya—she had gone to a play, *Abelard and Heloise,* and wouldn't be back for a while. I left a message at the desk for her to meet me at my car when she got back.

I walked around for a while, went to a pub and had an expensive half pint of lager, bought a few groceries, then came back to the car after dark and waited. I heard that Anya returned from the play at 11:00 or 11:30 p.m. and she finally met me at the car. We went into her hotel lobby and talked for a while. She had a busy schedule of lectures and tours but could spare a little time to break away. She was really impressed with England. Her Austrian bus driver had gotten lost in Oxford....

The narrative ends here. I do not exactly recall what happened afterward, but I do know that there was a problem with my getting a flight back. The Anglo-America Association completely dropped the ball and had no tickets waiting for me at the Seaglair office. I had to call my father and request an emergency loan so I could buy an airplane ticket back to Columbus, Ohio, since I was all out of money. Somehow he wired more cash to an American Express and I bought a ticket out of Heathrow.

I could not find anyone to buy my Austin A35, so I just left it in the Heathrow parking lot when I went there for the flight. I was originally supposed to travel back on September 9, but I do not recall when I was able to return, or where I stayed while I was waiting (in the car somewhere? Maybe). But thanks to my father, I made it back and the adventure was over.

When I got back to Ohio State University, I declared a journalism major. The first course I took, Journalism 101, taught me more about writing than I ever suspected I could learn. English literature classes teach you how to write to evoke a response or stimulate an emotion, but journalism classes teach you how to write to communicate. Expository prose became my new life adventure, and I've been an editor ever since.

The Big Trek, 1969

Wow! What an adventure! An American Odyssey—a saga of sensation and terror, destined to be told and re-told by minstrels and bards for generations to come—an experiment with life, a covenant with death, yea, a journey into the jaws of Hell that even devils fear to take. And *we* did it all. We, the Terrible Two: a pair of fearless conquerors who dared to attack the Unknown for the sake of pure thrill: Jocular George and Frank the Freak.

No one is safe when the Terrible Two are in town. So, barman hide your booze and farmer hide your daughter, because the Terrible Two are on the loose! Gentle reader, turn out the lights, ignite a couple of candles, snuggle in under the bedcovers, and shiver and cringe along with us as we take a hitchhiking trip across the United States.

Wednesday, August 27, 1969

Frank's real name was Frank Safranek, but his friends called him "Skit"—Skit Safranek (get it?). We left Columbus, Ohio, hitting the trail West, not knowing exactly where we were going, letting fortune carry us where it wished, blown by winds of fate, but at the same time heading in the general direction of either San Francisco or Seattle. The purposes of our journey were elementary ones: I to find a job and settle down to a life of relative innocuousness in some exotic landscape, and Frank to visit friends and seek adventure, both of which could be found in the two cities mentioned above. Our mode of travel was one which was accepted as valid in Europe, but which is looked down on in America—the gentle Art of Thumbing.

We set out on Route 40 at 8:30 a.m., just outside greater Columbus, Ohio. A friend of Frank's had given us a lift here, as it would have been difficult to find a ride within the city limits. We waited around for 20 minutes, cursing silently at cars that did not stop for us, until finally a car pulled up driven by a lone, middle-aged man. We subsequently learned, through intensive interrogation, that the guy was an itinerant gasoline salesman who was traveling to Springfield, Ohio, to ply his wares and make tons of money. We talked of gas and other combustibles along the way.

The salesman let us off on the west side of Springfield on Interstate 70 near an extremely encouraging entrance ramp, with many cars bearing California license plates passing us by in a westerly direction. At 9:25 a.m., two Ohio farmboys-turned-soldiers picked us up in a 1968 orange Camaro that was so cramped it barely held both us and our luggage. I was carrying a bedroll, a backpack, and an extremely heavy duffel bag containing everything I might need to live a few months out West. Frank had a bedroll and a small backpack.

These army boys, by the way, were a bit on the inebriated side and were guzzling some Johnny Walker while they weaved in and out of freeway traffic at what seemed to be 110 miles per hour. Death peered at us around every bend. These all-American GIs were headed for Dayton, Ohio, but they missed it by three exits due to being in a drunken stupor. We went our separate ways a few miles west of Dayton and started thumbing again on I-70 at an entrance ramp.

At 10:05 a.m., an Ohio Highway Patrolman picked us up. Unfortunately, he wasn't planning to give us a ride anywhere. He told us very paternalistically that it was illegal to hitchhike on Interstate highways. Well, it was technically illegal to thumb anywhere in any state. However, in some areas this was not enforced. Interstate thumbing was almost always enforced, although if hitchhikers are subtly placed on an entrance ramp, they may be overlooked. He added that we were grossly threatening national security by thumbing here, but that it was perfectly all right to do it on old Route 40 "a half mile" north, and that if he caught us again on an Interstate he would beat us up and take our money (or maybe he said he would arrest us). So we got off I-70 and walked a good two miles to Route 40, a lonely road going west. It was our biggest mistake.

After an hour of unproductive thumbing—with tears in our eyes bought on by the relentless persecution of an oppressive police force—we got a ride from a college student driving a Volkswagen. He was a pleasant sort of chap, and he informed us that what we had been thumbing on was Alternate Route 40, which jogged around for 15 miles or so before reaching the real Route 40. He said it would be tons better if we were on I-70, but if the Highway Patrol says no, then law and order must prevail. Frank and I were very fortunate to find this VW guy, because we would have been stuck in a suburban nowhere otherwise. He let us off on the real Route 40 at 11:00 a.m. near Vandalia, Ohio.

Real troubles now began. There was very little traffic on this road, and it was all local. After a while we caught a short ride to Arlington, Ohio, and found that we were in an even worse situation than before. Arlington is a mere crossroads of a town with a population of maybe a few hundred, most of whom were either dead or dying of old age. After another era of waiting with only an occasional car coming by and usually turning off north or south before reaching us, we caught another short ride to Lewisburg, Ohio, a bustling metropolis of 1,400 farmers and 1,400 head of cattle, where we again proceeded to thumb at 1:00 p.m., bewitched, bothered, and bewildered.

It was now 3:30 p.m. We had been standing along the road in front of a farmhouse outside Lewisburg for two-and-a-half hours with no success at all. I even tried flagging down a couple of cars, but they just veered into the left lane and sped by. For the past 20 minutes, the man who owned that farmhouse had been sitting on his porch and watching us. Suddenly he disappeared inside and came back a minute later with a shotgun and sat down again, continuing to watch us, but embellishing his scrutiny with curses that we were too far away to hear clearly, but were definitely ugly.

Frank thought he might be planning to shoot some blackbirds or something, but I was not so sure. When he started walking toward us, gun in hand, cursing vehemently, we saw the anger in his face, and we knew it wasn't birds that he was after. Luckily, before he got to us, his wife (or mother) ran up to him and cooled him off, taking him inside. At that point we decided it might be prudent to start walking for a while, and we did.

We had committed no crime. It was merely our looks that were objectionable (my beard and Frank's longish hair). If you have ever seen the movie *Easy Rider,* you will know the exact situation we were up against. Luckily, we did not see that movie until later that year, or we might have moved down the road a bit faster.

We walked and walked and walked. My duffel bag was heavier than ever and we had to take turns carrying it. After a couple of miles, we sauntered past a sort of suburban area with a few pre-fab houses along the side of the road. Here there was a man working in his garage who saw us go past, and he hailed us and asked us where we were going. We showed him our sign and said we were headed for the West Coast, and he pleasantly told us that he could give us a ride to an entrance ramp on Interstate 70 if we waited an hour or so while he fixed his car. We thanked him very much and accepted his offer, because in terms of footsoreness, I-70 was a good distance away.

We told him about our experience with the farmer and he said he wasn't surprised—Lewisburg is a strange town, he said, with a lot of narrow-minded people in it who don't particularly like strangers. He said that he and his wife had been living there for more than two years and they still were not accepted by the townsfolk. While the guy fixed his car, his wife prepared for us a delicious meal of beans and cornbread and it tasted really good. These people restored our faith in human nature. We vowed then and there never, never to leave the Interstate again.

After the man dropped us off at I-70, we soon got a ride at 5:50 p.m. from a red-haired ex-Navy officer who was traveling to Indianapolis with his 10-year-old son, an intelligent and inquisitive lad. Both of them were quite friendly, especially the kid, who asked us all sorts of questions about what we were going to do out west, and so forth.

The man was congenial during the first part of the ride, but he was drinking beer as he was driving. As we neared Indianapolis, his driving got progressively slower, and occasionally he would swerve. He also started yelling at the kid, who was beginning to criticize (albeit naively and with great affection) his dad's driving. Then the guy started talking about his wife who had divorced him, probably because he was an alcoholic, but this was only speculation on our part. He let us off on the east side of Indianapolis at 7:50 p.m., and our problem now was to get around to the west side of the city, no mean task.

We chatted with a guy at a nearby gas station who told us that the best way to get around the city was to take the Interstate 465 bypass, which was right next to the gas station. While we were thumbing at the entrance ramp, we became puzzled by the fact that there was very little traffic going onto I-465, although many cars were coming off it. We found out the reason at 8:10 p.m. when an asphalt truck picked us up. The driver said that 465 hadn't been completed for more than three miles or so, at which point it dead-ended.

We had been given a bum steer. However, we were extremely fortunate, because the asphalt guy went very much out of his way to give us a ride around the city (some 35 miles) through many jogs and detours, finally dropping us off around 10:00 p.m. outside Brownsburg, Indiana, on Interstate 74.

Frank and I found a Marathon gas station with a picnic area behind it and asked the manager if we could bed down there for the night. We slept, troubled by vaguely evil dreams.

Thursday, August 28, 1969

At the crack of dawn (6:00 a.m.), I woke Frank up and with a minimum of fooling around, we hit the road again. We seemed to be making terrible time, what with the big holdup on old Route 40 in Ohio. We then discovered that there was absolutely no traffic entering Interstate 74 from the ramp where we were standing, so we decided to take a chance and thumb on the freeway itself. (Those bold adventurers!)

Finally, at 7:15 a.m. we picked up a short, nine-mile ride to Lizton, Indiana, and found ourselves trapped in an out-of-the-way spot where no one would stop for us. Nonetheless, after an hour or so we caught a ride from a guy going somewhere in South Dakota. He said he could take us all the way to Omaha, Nebraska, if we were patient and waited an hour or two while he visited some old buddies at Chanute Air Force Base outside Champaign, Illinois. We said yes, we can be patient!

On the way to Champaign, he told us a bunch of wild, scary, entirely fabricated stories about things that had happened to him back in his own hitchhiking days. He also told us that we were lucky that he had picked us up, because it would have been hard getting a ride across Illinois, at the time notorious for its incomplete interstate highways.

We arrived in Champaign at 9:30 a.m. The guy said that since we did not have a pass to get onto the base, he would drop us and our gear off at a restaurant and meet us there in an hour after he got done chatting with his Air Force friends. He promised to returrn, because he wanted us to help him drive so he could make better time getting to South Dakota.

We sat in the restaurant for a while, amusing ourselves by writing letters to our respective girlfriends back in Columbus. We waited an hour, then we hauled our luggage out to the edge of the road and waited some more. Then we started pacing furiously out of frustration. After another hour had passed, we concluded that the old so-and-so would not be returning as scheduled. We swore bitterly and prayed that his cowardly fat would be rendered in the deepest circles of Hell.

At 11:30 a.m. we started thumbing on Interstate 74 outside the restaurant. Our problems were not over. While we had been waiting for the guy to come back, two girls had walked up from the restaurant and positioned themselves near us on the freeway entrance ramp. They were thumbing to somewhere in Wisconsin. We told them that west was the wrong way to go if they wanted to get to Wisconsin, but they just sneered and said that they wished to avoid Chicago, as conditions there were ripe for either getting lost, stranded, or waylaid. So they were thumbing west, then north.

We admired their logic but wished that they would get to Wisconsin with the greatest possible speed, as their presence was detrimental to our getting a ride. They obviously would have priority if anyone stopped.

To complicate matters further, a policeman cruised by and blared at us with his loudspeaker, telling all four of us to get off the road, that it was illegal to hitchhike anywhere in Illinois, and we

should all walk. We said we were very sorry, officer, but we didn't
know, and that we would very humbly catch a bus in town and
leave the state. After the cop left, we started hitchhiking again.
About 10 minutes later, we saw a flashing red light in the distance,
and for the next few seconds we frantically thrust our thumbs out
at approaching cars, beseeching them with all the ESP that we
could muster that we desperately needed a ride.

We finally caught a ride from a mustached guy in a
delivery truck just in the nick of time. The same cop was coming
around the corner to check up on us. The two girls were not so
fortunate—apparently they were either picked up and either hauled
down to a bus station or given a ride up the freeway to the county
line. We never found out which. However, later on in
Bloomington, Illinois, we saw them thumbing north.

The delivery truck dropped us off in Mahomet, Illinois, at
1:00 p.m. Interstate 74 was not completed at Mahomet, nor was it
completed anywhere else in western Illinois except for a small
stretch at Peoria. We were thus compelled to take to the back
roads.

We caught a ride almost immediately on US Highway 150
from a college student driving a Volkswagen. He was headed for
Bloomington, Illinois, and said that he would drop us off on the far
side of town at a particularly productive hitchhiking spot that he
knew about.

He dropped us off, but the spot (on US Highway 51) was
not a good one at all. We waited around until 3:00 p.m., then we
started to cry as raging seas are wont to roar. However, just then a
middle-aged man who sold farm equipment picked us up and said
he would take us a good 60 miles to La Salle, Illinois, where we
could catch Interstate 80 west. This salesman was an exceedingly
good-natured fellow who never raised his voice, but he was rather
unlettered and politically conservative. He started talking politics
with us, but we shied away from arguing with him because we
didn't want to get dumped out of the car at some uninhabited
region of Illinois.

In La Salle we picked up a ride at 4:20 p.m. from two farm
boys in a beat-up 1961 Chevy. Frank and I were both pretty tired,
and the farm boys were not too talkative, so we dozed most of the

way. I must mention here that the scenery in Illinois is unusual, although very ugly and boring at the same time. Imagine an ocean of corn ranging in every direction as far as the earth's curvature permits one to view it, with an indistinguishable merging of sky and land at the horizon. And this goes on for miles and miles and miles with no break except for an occasional farmhouse or billboard—no trees, hills, rocks, or anything else. I thought Ohio was bad until I saw central Illinois.

The farm boys took us to Moline, Illinois, which is right across the river from Iowa. We were still on Interstate 80. We spotted two girl hitchhikers on the same ramp as we were. They were upstream traffic-wise from us and were considerably diminishing the probability of our getting a ride. However, we saw a black car pull up alongside them, and just after that a small foreign car pulled up in back of the black car. It turned out that the black car was a policeman and that the foreign car was driven by a couple guys who saw that the girls needed a ride and were getting apprehended. So the guys apparently worked things out with the cop and gave the girls a lift.

We found all this out because the same policeman picked us up a few minutes later. He was very understanding and gave us a ride to a freeway ramp near the Iowa border so that Illinois wouldn't have us on its hands anymore. At this point I noticed that my duffel bag (made out of cheap plastic) was horribly ripped and getting more damaged each time we got into and out of cars. Nothing was tumbling out yet, but my stuff was in peril of getting lost.

We got a short ride across the Mississippi River into Davenport, Iowa, at 6:10 p.m. This was the first time I had seen the Mississippi. It was rather disappointing—not as muddy or sluggish as I'd expected from Mark Twain. Anyway, we soldiers of fortune were now in another fix: It was getting late and we were in a bad position for thumbing on the east side of Davenport.

However, luck was with us once more and a Volkswagen van stopped for us. The two hippies who were driving it, Hugh and Mike, said that they were going to Denver, Colorado. This was our first big break! All our rides up until now had been small, local ones, which is why we were making such lousy time. Hugh and

Mike were rather agreeable lads who hailed from Stockbridge, Massachusetts (the home of Alice's Restaurant made famous by Arlo Guthrie) and were headed west to seek the meaning of life. We discussed politics, religion, philosophy, music, and other college-type subjects the entire time we were with them—a pleasant respite from chatting about the weather with corn-fed country folks.

We had a meager dinner at some truck stop in Iowa that offered some excellent bread (most truck stops had excellent food in those days) and I bought some masking tape for $2.00 with which I repaired my duffel bag. It was the most I spent on any one day during the trip west.

Friday, August 29, 1969

Hugh and Mike were driving non-stop all night, just as they had done the previous nights coming from Massachusetts. They were very hardy chaps—I still don't see how they managed it.

At half-past midnight, while breezing through western Iowa, we got a flat tire. There was a jack in the back of the van, but for some reason it didn't work, and we couldn't get the tire far enough off the ground to change it. So Hugh lit a flare and walked off down the road, hoping to flag down a car or truck that could give him a ride to the nethermost gas station. We watched as about 10 cars ignored both Hugh's flare and his flagging.

Finally, a small truck came along and gave him a ride to a gas station. He came back later with a gas station attendant who had a decent jack, and he put the spare on for us. Then we followed him back to the station so he could patch the old tire and put it back on. We got moving again at 2:45 a.m. and reached Omaha, Nebraska, at 7:30 a.m.

At noon, we pulled off the freeway onto a rural Nebraska road and stopped for a picnic and some fun. There were a bunch of spiny-type locust trees nearby and Mike borrowed my knife to cut some of the spines off. He said he wanted to make a Jesus hat. We had a pretty wild time.

Frank and I had to decide whether we wanted to go to Denver with Hugh and Mike, taking the southern route to California, then north along the coast to Seattle; or take the northern route, getting let off at US Highway 26 or something in Nebraska, from which we could take I-25 and I-90 north to Washington. We finally decided to try the northern route.

Hugh and Mike dropped us off at Ogallala, Nebraska, at 3:00 p.m. Again, the situation looked bad. We were despairing of ever getting out of the Great Plains when a car pulled up. It contained two women who were headed to Loveland, Colorado, which is some 40 miles north of Denver. This was not exactly the direction we wanted to go, but we accepted the ride because it would be getting late soon and we could follow Interstate 25 north at Loveland.

The women were about 35, married, and schoolteachers who lived in Ogallala and went shopping in Loveland, ostensibly because prices were lower there. We had a very pleasant ride through eastern Colorado with them. They followed the Platte River and US Highways 138, 6, and 34 to Loveland. This is the area where the high plains meet the foothills and the result is a kind of rugged, sparsely vegetated, hilly area that would make a good set for filming Westerns. When they dropped us off at Loveland at 7:00 p.m. it began to rain—our first of the trip.

In the midst of a moderate drizzle, Frank and I ran up to the entrance ramp on Interstate 25. Almost before we got there, a car stopped with two girls in it, this time unmarried and 18 or 19 years of age. They were going to Sheridan, Wyoming, and they just *hated* to see two such handsome examples of masculinity standing out in the cold, cold rain with no shelter in sight. Sheridan was again a bit out of the way for us, as we then planned to follow I-80 west from Cheyenne, Wyoming, to Portland, Oregon. Sheridan was, we supposed, way too far north. So after conversing platonically with the girls for a few miles, they let us off at Cheyenne at 8:00 p.m., cold and shivering in the now-pouring rain.

We marched through the slush a quarter mile to a gas station where we wandered around dazed and confused for a few minutes. Finally, a blond crew-cut guy in a brand-new Volkswagen pulled up, and we asked him where he was going. He said he was

146

headed for Billings, Montana, and he offered to give us a ride. We accepted, figuring it was our only chance for survival, and that we could take Interstate 90 from Billings straight through to Seattle. We left right away (about 8:30 p.m.) and drove north all night.

I'm glad we got a ride because it was raining heavily—things that love night love not such nights as these. It turned out that this crew-cut guy used to be a bearded, long-haired liberal type of person before the army got him, so we talked about music and politics and other hip topics. The guy was of Swedish descent and his name was Gunnar, of all things. He never stopped talking about Billings, Montana, and how absolutely great the country and the people were up there. Trouble was that he kept talking to us all night when we were trying to go to sleep, and we had to take turns staying up to listen to him talk so that he could stay awake enough to drive. The roads through Wyoming (mostly freeways) were very deserted at that time of night; it was very desolate foothill country. We were dead tired when we pulled into Billings at 3:30 a.m.

Frank and I landed ourselves in an all-night restaurant in Billings and had doughnuts and coffee until sunrise. The people in the restaurant were so friendly! If this restaurant had been in Illinois or Indiana, people would have looked at us askance and muttered insults at us underneath their breath and given us lousy service; but *this* restaurant was in Montana, and the waitress came up and chatted with us while we were sipping coffee, and the table-cleaning boy sat down and talked for a while. It's a different country out there.

A word about Billings: It's a very beautiful town built underneath a cliff, on top of which there is a copper mine and an airport, while on the other side of town is the Yellowstone River. Most of the town is park, while the rest is very frontierish and rugged, while at the same time somewhat intellectual, with two colleges. I have vowed to visit Billings again less transiently sometime when I can take a longer look at it.

Saturday, August 30, 1969

At 6:00 a.m., Frank and I hit Interstate 80. Traffic was sparse, but we found a short ride up the freeway with a family going to Laurel, Montana. There was no traffic at all at Laurel. We waited around for an hour or so, twiddling our thumbs until an occasional car came along, whereupon we stuck them out. We finally got a ride from a Montana hippie driving a VW who was traveling to Missoula, Montana, about 330 miles up the road.

When we left Laurel we entered the "foothills" that were larger than most peaks I was familiar with in the Pennsylvania Appalachians. The VW guy said that a lot of this land was still being sold cheaply by the government with the catch that the owner must show an improvement of at least $100 per year thus homesteaded. In other words, you have to start a farm or factory or mine or something if you want to keep the land.

After coming to Butte, Montana, we got into the *real* Rockies, the continental divide. There are just no words to describe the scenery: gigantic mountains; cascading waters; whispering pines; pig, cattle, and horse ranches; restaurants advertising buffalo burgers; sharply defined valleys with small mining towns dotted randomly at the bottom. Unspeakably majestic!

We were dropped off in Missoula at 2:30 p.m., where a carload of Indians picked us up. There were three men, two women, and one baby; all of them were extremely friendly and generous and tons of fun to talk to.

However, after a while the men started drinking beer. The driver had an unusual habit of having to smoke a cigarette after every bottle of beer—but then when he finished the cigarette his mouth was dry and he had to have another beer. One of the other men just went to sleep, while the other guy got a little less friendly and more introverted after a while. I had made friends with him prior to his getting a bit drunk, and since I wished to maintain this relationship, I carefully edited my remarks and responses. After some time, I didn't have to worry because he fell asleep sprawled all over the front seat and anyone who was sitting there. They all had to stop at a restroom every 10 minutes.

The women were rightfully scared they might drive off the side of a mountain, and there was ample opportunity for doing this, as the country between Missoula and Coeur d'Alene, Idaho, was some of the ruggedest I've seen. The driver was getting more rambunctious as we neared Spokane, Washington, and we had to stop to fix a flat tire once, which slowed us down a bit. Anyway, after a thrilling, scenic, and quite scary ride, they dropped us off at Spokane around 8:30 p.m.

Since thumbing was strictly prohibited in Washington State, we had to be careful about where we were standing. It was getting rather late, and we were anxious to get to Seattle as soon as possible, so we even looked into the possibility of taking a bus. However, we decided to try hitchhiking near the freeway.

We discovered that there were about three other groups of hitchhikers all going in the same direction to Seattle. Frank ran up to them and asked them what was going on. They said that they were all going to a rock festival in Seattle that weekend, similar to the one at Woodstock in New York.

Our spirits high and our metabolisms low, we managed to catch a ride for $1.00 apiece to Tacoma, Washington, from some pseudo-hippies going to the music festival. We slept almost all the way, not even noticing when a cop stopped them for speeding. We found out about it later. We also slept through the Cascade Mountains, although I managed to wake up every once in a while just in time to catch sight of some wildlife (deer, foxes, raccoons) that had been caught in the car's headlights.

Sunday, August 31, 1969

We arrived in Tacoma at 3:00 a.m. and got dropped off at a bourgeoise teenage restaurant named Denny's. People gave us sly looks and made derogatory remarks as we came in. We were now concerned about getting a ride into Seattle (about 30 miles away) since Kody (Frank's friend who lived there) was feeling sick and could not pick us up or greet us warmly.

When we were just about ready to give up, we were saved by two beautiful girls, Jeanne and Val, who felt sorry for us. They gave us a ride into town, bringing us all the way to Kody's doorstep. They even invited us to come with them to the rock festival on Monday, but we declined. Kody and Craig (her husband) greeted us somewhat sleepily as we arrived at their house around 4:00 a.m. I finally got to sleep around 5:00, but Frank stayed up telling his life story because he had insomnia.

Later in the morning, Kody and Craig and Chère and Nancy (two of Kody's friends) and Frank and I went to the Sky River Rock Festival and Lighter Than Air Faire near Tacoma. It was a magnificent experience. Everything was just like Woodstock a mere two weeks earlier, but without the bad weather and the mud, and with plenty of food and sanitation and thousands of hippies in various stages of dishabille. There were all sorts of groovy rock bands there, and we stayed all day listening to the best music the 1960s had to offer.

I cannot remember exactly which bands we heard, but there were plenty at that festival, including Santana, Country Joe and the Fish, Ramblin' Jack Elliot, Buffy Sainte-Marie, the Peanut Butter Conspiracy, the Youngbloods, John Fahey, and It's a Beautiful Day. It was every bit as exceptional as Woodstock, with legendary musicians, happy freaks tripping out, and an overwhelming sense of community. And no one died, as far as I know.

Then we all went back to Craig's house.

That is the end of the diary. I found an apartment in Seattle so that I could look for a job, and I even applied at the *Seattle Post-Intelligencer* as a copyeditor. However, there were few jobs of any kind available because the Boeing plant had just laid off a few thousand workers. The job market was glutted. I gave up after nearly two weeks of frustration and returned to Columbus and more classes at Ohio State University.

The Long Haul, 1970

Let me weave a tale of nerve-wracking, heart-lancing, adrenaline-stimulating adventure—a saga of courage unparalleled in even the most heroic of times—a narrative so fraught with terror and imminent peril that lesser men will fail to repress a shudder while reading its crimson pages. The heroes of this history are three:

Jocular George — a menace to sanity, he reduces all he sees and hears to gibberish, irrelevance, and absurdity.

Treacherous Tom — the scourge of all Establishments and the bane of all dictators; as he approaches, the windows of no capitalistic enterprise go unbroken.

Psilocybin Sally — her pleasure is pot and her law is love; nothing she smokes can get her too high.

Embark with me now on a voyage to the inner depths of consciousness, where the secret forces of the id are released in a whirlwind of wicked thoughts and the subliminal desires of countless ages are unleashed brutally on an unprepared world. Come with me now on The Long Haul!

Saturday, September 5, 1970

After eating an unhurried, delightful meal at Tom's house and packing all the necessary provisions and equipment into the back of his matchless off-white Mustang, Tom and I set off on our journey slightly after midnight, saying somewhat prolonged goodbyes to Tom's parents, sister, and dogs.

Tom, who was a co-worker at the Riverside Methodist Hospital in Columbus, Ohio, was the first to drive, as I had had a grueling, tormented day working at the hospital and wanted to sleep for a while. Nothing of immense importance occurred during the night except when we crossed into Indiana from Ohio. There at the border, Tom (who is as a rule quite perceptive) observed a huge arch stretching across the highway, the obverse side of which welcomed people to that state of opportunity, Ohio. It was erected by Gov. Jim Rhodes before he lost the gubernatorial primary and it fell into disuse after that. By daybreak, we had reached Effingham, Illinois, where we loaded our ice chest with Coke and our gas tank with fuel, then I drove all the way to Altamont before we had discovered we had left the Coke-filled ice chest back at the gas station. Cursing such an evil day, we had to drive back to get it.

We ate an uneventful lunch near Pacific, Missouri, where we got suspicious looks from waitresses. We purchased some radio batteries from a general store so we could listen to some music, but the heaviest tones that were available on AM radio were Roy Acuff Jr. and Theresa Brewer.

We obtained more gas and bad vibes from a redneck Shell station in Lebanon, Missouri, around noon, then stopped in Springfield to check out the centers of radical political activity which, we found to our dismay, were quite non-existent. Tom bought some sunglasses while I lurked ominously around town. Thoroughly disgusted, we stalked back to the car and sped out of the place before we were beaten up or anything.

Pressing ever onward, we drove straight through Tulsa and Oklahoma City and consumed a luxuriant dinner at a sterling establishment in El Reno, Oklahoma, known as Hensley's Restaurant. The people were courteous and so was the food. Since it was getting late, we decided to bed down at a place outside of Clinton, Oklahoma, known as the Foss Reservoir Recreation Area. The weather was warm and a vigorous breeze was blowing as we camped out 'neath the Oklahoma stars and slept a dreamless sleep.

Sunday, September 6, 1970

I woke up around 6:30 a.m. and roused Tom, who lay snoring abed at my side. I piled Tom and our gear into the car and drove off into the West, bent on reaching Santa Fe, New Mexico, by early afternoon.

We trucked on into Amarillo, Texas, where a hippie who worked at a gas station told us that the town was a police state and that we'd better watch our speed or else we'd be in big trouble. We thanked him very kindly, then drove on down the road and ate breakfast in a Denny's Restaurant.

Around this time, we started to develop problems with the alignment of the front wheels, so we stopped in Tucumcari, New Mexico, to have them fixed, but either no one had the proper equipment or they charged too much for the service. The scenery was starting to get hillier now, instead of the flat plains we had to put up with in Oklahoma and Texas. Tom, not ever having seen real mountains before, was visibly awed and wondered aloud at the splendor and the imposition of the arid, sagebrushed peaks and mesas we saw scattered around the horizon. Having grown up in sight of the Blue Ridge Mountains, I laughed in derision.

We pulled into Santa Fe at about 12:20 p.m. and drove to a place called The Center, which was where we were supposed to meet Psilocybin Sally either today or Monday.

Sally had been staying in a commune for several months, but she wanted to travel to California with us and get a ride back to Columbus to continue taking classes at Ohio State University. The Center was an extensive, adobe crash pad for transient freaks run by one Father George, a Catholic priest with liberal ideas and a long, black, Karl Marx–like beard that sprouted from under his prominent nose like the tamarisks on Mount Sinai.

We contacted the Rev himself, who informed us that Sally had not yet come in from the commune house she was staying in at El Rito, a village about 40 miles north of Santa Fe. We walked around town for a while, looking unproductively for a good auto mechanic, then got bored and decided to drive up to El Rito ourselves to see if we could catch Sally before she left. We drove up into the mountains, the Mustang groaning at every turn, smoked a joint that some girl had thrown out of a car at us in Santa Fe, and finally found the commune, only to discover that Sally had left there about the same time we had left Santa Fe.

So, after getting a brief tour of the premises by Bob and Carla, the only remaining freaks in the place, we went back to Santa Fe, where we joined Sally and four of her commune friends, three of whom left to go somewhere in Ohio (of all places), leaving the other (named Ozone) at The Center. Ozone walked around a bit with us and borrowed some money and conversed superficially about his alternative lifestyle.

Since Ozone wished to go to Ann Arbor, Michigan, sometime or other, we said that we would give him a ride when the three of us came through to return to Columbus.

At The Center we had a dinner consisting of something vaguely reminiscent of rancid cornbread. Then the four of us left to go to a festival that the Chicanos were having at the Plaza in honor of some battle the Spanish lost somewhere, and we walked around and looked at the people and ate tortillas and laughed at the fatuity of life.

Then we came back and crashed in an empty house that no one had lived in since there was a murder there a month or two previously. A guy named Chicken was staying there, plus his friends Tinker and Barb. We smoked dope and sang songs and nodded out to the sound of Chicken playing merry rondelets on his guitar.

Monday, September 7, 1970

I woke up earlier than the rest of the hippies that were sleeping there and, rather than sitting around, decided to saunter around the outskirts of town to see if there were a mountain or two that warranted climbing. I found one, climbed it, looked down upon the city and saw that it was good, then climbed back down.

When I returned at 9:00 a.m., almost everyone was awake, or at least pretending to be. We made some coffee, took warm baths, collected our luggage, bid farewell to Chicken and his friends, told Ozone we'd meet him on September 16, and took off, three adventurers with one thought in mind—to reap the harvest of life before the predators of death caught up with it.

We stopped in Gallup, New Mexico, to see what could be done about our balding tires and mal-aligned wheels, and Tom bought a used tire to replace one that had been giving us no end of trouble. This solved things temporarily, but worse perils were to follow.

We drove on into Arizona heading for the Grand Canyon when I decided that we wanted to see the Barringer Meteor Crater near Winslow, which was right on the way to wherever it was we were going. We arrived there about 5:00 p.m., eager to delve into all sorts of meteoritic lore. The price for observing this astronomical oddity was atrocious, but our enthusiasm would not be dampened. We paid the highwayman at the gate and passed on to examine one of the greatest cosmic wonders in the history of our planet. There was a winding, narrow path leading down to the bottom of the crater, marked only by confusing yellow arrows. Sally (that intrepid soul!) climbed with us down to the bottom and back in bare feet, putting Tom and me to shame.

At the very bottom of the crater lay several mine shafts where Daniel Barringer had tried to find the mass of the original meteorite, all to no avail.

The view from the bottom of the crater was quite an impressive sight. I remarked that it would be appropriate to stage a play by Sophocles or Aeschylus there; Tom observed that it might be fun to have a rock festival; while Sally shouted that she sure wished she had some acid she could drop because the place was so groovy, wow.

The climb back up was a long one, but we made it by sundown and drove on to the Grand Canyon to spend the night. The restaurant they had there was too plush for our tastes, so we settled for some arid spaghetti and alkaline potatoes in the cafeteria. Then we drove into the campgrounds past a sign that said "Full," found a spot where nobody else was, got out the sleeping bags, said our lay-me-downs, and fell into a deep, comatose state.

Tuesday, September 8, 1970

Sally arose at dawn and woke the rest of us up after mumbling some mantric hymns. We hurriedly got our stuff together and raced along the canyon rim so that we would be able to see the sunrise shedding its golden rays into the spacious canyon.

We reached Hopi Point, where a few other people had gathered with similar motives. To avoid the thronging masses, the three of us climbed out on an outjutting rock to observe the spectacular vista surrounding us. It was truly awesome—a chasm fit for poets and balladeers to sing about for all time. The sun sparkled and shimmered on the red and yellow canyon walls, chasing the gray shadows away from their rocky lairs. We noticed that some freak had carved a peace sign on an outcrop of rock about 30 feet below us—how he managed to do that is beyond me.

After the sun rose, we hiked down to the snack bar and got something to eat, then marched to the store to buy foodstuffs for the long journey we were about to undertake in the canyon. We started down the Kaibab Trail at 10:00 a.m., armed only with a knapsack full of food and a small canteen. The trail was not so rough as the one at Meteor Crater, and it was not at all difficult to go down. As a matter of fact, Sally ran most of the way, leaving the less irresponsible members of our party behind cursing at her folly.

The trail was traveled by freaks other than ourselves, including a party of 20 or so from England and a couple of guys prospecting for peyote cactus. We traveled about 3½ miles before we were able to see the Colorado River and hear its roaring rapids; at which point we decided to stop and eat lunch whilst viewing the panoramic display of color that presented itself.

Lunch was a fabulous assortment of peaches, plums, berry pies, and chocolate milk, all of which we wolfed down eagerly to fortify ourselves for the treacherous journey back. It took us three long, terror-filled hours to get back to the top of the rim. Plagued by cactus thorns, oppressed by the heat, beset by hordes of rabid desert lizards, suffering from dehydration and our exhausted anoxic muscles, we finally groped our way to the top—a few hours older yet many years wiser. A hot shower greeted us back at the camp—it was as rain on the parched desert of our souls.

Our new plan was to make San Francisco by next morning. But first we had to do something about the tires, which were feeling the effects of our long sojourn. We buzzed down to a gas station in Williams, Arizona, where we bought a used tire and got it fitted.

Sally and I walked around town to a shop called The Goldmine, where I benevolently bought her two brightly colored kerosene lamps. I got myself an inexpensive book of Beat writings by William S. Burroughs, Jack Kerouac, and others, but it bummed Sally out because it wasn't happy and optimistic like a hippie book should be.

We had not driven 60 more miles when the tire Tom had bought in Williams came apart due to it being only a retread and no good at all. We had to creep down the road to another gas station and get the thing fixed before we could proceed any further. We discussed returning to Williams on our way back to Columbus to give a stern talking-to to the guy who had sold it to us, or at least chastise him moderately. Finally, we reached the Mojave Desert and drove through its arid vastnesses at dead of night to spare the car's cooling system, stopping once in Barstow, California, to get the tires balanced.

Wednesday, September 9, 1970

Through my unique and uncanny ability to stay awake while driving, even to the point of mortality, we arrived in Paso Robles, California, at about 7:30 a.m. We had a breakfast of hotcakes at a plush restaurant, then traveled on up the road to San Francisco, seedbed of liberality in a desert of conservatism. The sight of that city as we first entered it will never cease to amaze me—every time I think back on it, it kinda makes me misty.

Tom drove us around the city to get a general view of it first, and then we headed across the Golden Gate Bridge to find some sort of beach where we could swim. After driving along a strange, winding road that crept across hills and valleys of unparalleled splendor, we chanced upon a free beach on the Pacific coast called Muir Beach. The water was freezing, but this did not stop Tom from making an heroic plunge into its icy grasp. Later on I waded in after gathering up courage, but Sally refused to go in until we walked down the beach further where there were a bunch of naked freaks swimming and sunbathing and playing frisbee, whereupon she flung off all her clothes and threw herself into the brine.

We lazed on the beach for a few hours, watching and talking to naked people, then we headed back to take a look at Cliff House back in San Francisco, which is where Tom thought we might be able to crash for a while. It wasn't really too much, just a lookout point on the shore with a big parking lot.

Then we drove down further south past the Haight-Ashbury district, which apparently isn't what it used to be in 1966, but there were a bunch of hippies there and some head shops. Then we went to a grocery store and bought some food and ate it on the beach on the city's Pacific coast.

By this time, it was almost sunset, and since Sally wanted to see this grand occurrence from a particularly scenic spot, we drove out to Golden Gate Bridge again and started walking across it—only to find (to our great dismay) that the west side was closed to sun-watching pedestrians. So, bummed out, we went back to Cliff House and watched the sun dip out of sight into the fog that was creeping up the coast, while the waves crashed into the rocky cliff below us. A cathartic sight, indeed.

That night we drove across the Bay Bridge into Berkeley where we looked around some of the head shops that were still open. We decided to stay at the Berkeley Hotel, a reputable establishment run by a quite conscientious proprietor who was only slightly perturbed about Sally (an unmarried type of person) staying with us at the hotel. So, after buzzing around Berkeley for a while, we slept and showered at the hotel for a nominal $10.50.

Thursday, September 10, 1970

Sally and I spent most of the day visiting various shops in the Berkeley area, while Tom drove around San Francisco looking for hospitals to check out to see if any were worth working at. The two most likely prospects were Franklin and Kaiser, both of which paid pretty well for male attendants and surgical techs and had no

prohibitions on long hair. Tom told them they'd probably hear
from us again in March, if not before.

In Berkeley, I bought several cheap books on occult topics
and a William Blake poster, while Sally copped some incense from
a black Hare Krishna guy who was chanting and dancing and
playing exotic instruments right there on the street. She also
bought a small bell that she now wears continually on a band
around her ankle. This was a very good idea because now we can
keep track of her when she wanders off on tangential excursions on
her own, as she is wont to do.

We discovered that Tom had gotten a parking ticket, but we
paid it no mind because, after all, parking tickets are just a minor
expression of the tyranny of the capitalistic military-industrial
complex that permeates every aspect of our society and to which
the forces of freedom, namely us, are eternally opposed.

That night, after rearranging the car to allow more freedom
of movement, we motored down to Fisherman's Wharf for a
sumptuous repast of lobster and swordfish at a fancy restaurant
called Castagnola's, where we were attended to by a French maître
d' who was addicted to executing gallic flourishes and writing on
tablecloths. After satiating our rapacious appetites, we skeptically
went to see the Ripley Believe It or Not Museum and returned, not
believing that Robert Ripley could have made so much money
from exploiting reality, which is unbelievable by definition.

We then set out in quest of a place to sleep, no mean task.
We asked a number of longhairs in the Grant Street district where a
good place to crash was, but they stared at us vacantly and referred
us to the Switchboard phone number, which we had already tried,
but it was busy. We puttered about for hours, talking to freaks, taxi
drivers, nudie-show hawkers, and derelicts, but learned nothing
encouraging.

Hoping to find a spot by the highway north of San
Francisco, we headed across the Golden Gate Bridge again, only to
be accosted by an impenetrable fog that arose from the bay and
spread up the mountains. Fatigued to the point of prostration, Tom
with an herculean effort drove nearly to Petaluma, stopping only
occasionally for a few minutes of rest. But it was all for nought.
We couldn't sleep outside in the fog because it was too wet, and

we couldn't get away from the fog no matter where we went. It was a vicious circle. So we wound up sleeping all cramped up in the car in the midst of a thick and oppressive San Francisco fog.

Friday, September 11, 1970

Upon waking, we drove south to a place called Novato to have some new shock absorbers installed in the Mustang, after which we bumplessly journeyed back to San Francisco, where we walked around Chinatown buying obscure and inedible oriental foodstuffs.

We also went to the famed City Lights bookstore, where I bought a book from whom I believe to have been the man himself, Lawrence Ferlinghetti, whose plays and poetry are indelibly etched into the annals of art. From there the three of us took a hair-raising ride on a trolley car, where we met a black trolley-car driver who said he was part Chinese and who showed Sally how to steer and brake the trolley. I was suspicious of his motives, but I heroically refrained from cautioning him from further tutelage whilst leering maliciously from a shadowy corner of the car.

After buying some more posters and a Tarot deck at another head shop, we bid a last farewell to San Francisco and headed south for Big Sur, 100 miles or so along the coast. Reaching it around 10:00 p.m. or so, we found that the campgrounds were filled up with itinerant tourists on a weekend outing. Disgusted, we found a spot along the side of California State Route 1 (the Hippie Highway) that overlooked the tumultuous shore of the grand Pacific pounding against the land that stood in its watery way.

Saturday, September 12, 1970

Sally and I arose early to clean up and rearrange all our gear in the car. Tom did not get up until several policemen came along and started scanning the coastline below us with their binoculars. I asked them what they thought they were doing, and they replied that someone had called in to report a car going off the cliff not far from where we were camped. I expressed my best wishes for a successful search and told them I thought it was admirable that the police force here was actually doing something constructive, instead of going around kicking shit out of longhairs and capturing people in the act of smoking weed. They laughed and said modestly that they were just doing their job, kid.

Tom and Sally and I then ventured back to Big Sur, where we ate brunch at a restaurant owned and operated by somewhat inefficient freaks. The food was good, but the service was faulty. We bathed at the campground shower house and played on the swings with a little girl who was camping in the area. I taught her a few tricks she'd never seen before.

After Big Sur, we headed down the coast and made it to Santa Barbara at nightfall, where there is a branch of the University of California campus. This is the place where the local Bank of America branch was burned down in a protest of capitalistic monopoly.

We ate a delicious meal at a delicatessen, wandered around several freak shops, went over to the local Switchboard, and found a place to sleep for the night. It seems this dude named Jim had the lucky job of cleaning house for the manager of an apartment house in the area, and while the cat was away, so to speak, any freaks in the neighborhood who needed a place to sleep were welcome to stay. So we slept there in a nice semi-furnished apartment with several other hippies from Illinois, all of whom were generous with the dope they were smoking. We slept a long, dream-filled sleep.

Sunday, September 13, 1970

We bade farewell to our new Santa Barbara friends and cruised south toward Los Angeles. The first beach we hit was Manhattan Beach, one of the less popular surf beaches, but well-known enough to be mentioned in one or two Beach Boys songs. Out of pure kindness and generosity, I bought Sally a greeting card to send to her dad, on which was depicted a meek, wizened little old lady sitting uncomfortably next to a wired-out, deep-fat-fried, acid freak. Quite appropriate for Sally's dad.

We basked in the warm sun, frolicked in the cold, polluted water, and pondered the nature of life and existence. Sally and I walked quite a way down the shore on our left to take a look at an interesting pier belonging to some chemical company, but we got chased off by a guard because, after all, private property is sacred. Little did we know at the time that if we had chosen to walk down to the other pier on our right, we might have met Frank Safranek, a compeer of mine from Columbus who had accompanied me on The Big Trek to Seattle in 1969. He was staying at an apartment on the beach with some friends, but we did not hear about it until we got back to Columbus.

Later on, we ate a good greasy American dinner at a Colonel Sanders, then drove around searching, as usual, for a place to sleep. We drove down past Laguna Beach along the coast but found no place that would be unhassled by cops. We finally found a spot along a secondary highway that seemed barely adequate—it was a dirt road of sorts that really went nowhere and seemed merely to serve as a shortcut for construction vehicles to avoid the intersection. We parked the car so that it was partially hidden from the road, crawled into the bushes, and slept, tormented by sand fleas.

Monday, September 14, 1970

I woke up around 6:00 a.m. to the sound of a police siren going "schwoop," somewhat like the noise produced by a paranoid anemic turtle afflicted with hemorrhoids and chronic constipation. The law enforcement agents were upon us, enforcing the law.

Two Orange County sheriffs got out of their car and strutted up to us, shouting "Good morning!" very sarcastically, then asked us if we would be so gracious as to show them our IDs and any marijuana we might have with us. We said nastily that we had left our IDs in our Sunday pants and that we had smoked all our grass the night before and all we had left was heroin. Then we spat on their crisp, new uniforms and picked up dung cakes on the road and hurled them, all the time calling them swine and barbarians unfit for walking upon God's sacred earth.

No, actually, that's not true. We smiled very meekly and showed them our IDs, saying that even though we *looked* like we were liberal, we actually weren't, and we didn't smoke "pot" (as the hippies called it) because we were afraid of addiction, chromosome damage, and sterility. The sheriffs said that was very nice, that they were really very *good* cops, and that they wouldn't destroy *too* much of our property as they illegally ransacked our car for contraband.

One of the sheriffs was a young guy who had watched too many *Adam 12* shows. He kept making irrelevant, immature statements and sick jokes about the "dope-crazed Commie preverts" that infested Orange County. Well, they didn't find the small amount of grass we *did* have (in Sally's purse in an envelope) and they said they wouldn't arrest us 'cause we were decent guys who were from out of town and didn't know any better not to sleep alongside the road because there wasn't anywhere else to go.

Sally, Tom, and I then motored into Laguna Beach to do some laundry, after which we went down to Huntington Beach (which is where Surfer Joe went for the Annual Surfers' Convention Meet) to swim and sun ourselves for a while. Tom was having more car trouble, so he went off to look for a good gas station while Sally and I played in the sand and waded.

When Tom got back an hour or two later, he brought back a joint that a hitchhiker had given him and we smoked it there on the beach, which was rather deserted because school had already started and the weather was so cold.

After eating an all-American meal at a nearby McDonald's, we decided to take a drive down the Sunset Strip to see what downtown L.A. was all about. We saw all sorts of incredible sights, such as the original Brown Derby Restaurant, the Head East, the main Jesse Unruh for Governor headquarters (he was campaigning that year against Ronald Reagan for the job), Beverly Hills and its hillbillies, a couple of movie studios, and a whole bunch of plastic, chromium-plated people. We did not go into any of these places for various reasons, all of them good.

Now we again had trouble finding a place to sleep. Finally, we pulled into Doheny State Beach, which had camping facilities for people like us. It was closed, but this did not deter us. We drove into the camp and plopped down on an empty camping place.

Tuesday, September 15, 1970

We woke up quite early but, alas, not early enough. The ranger (who had just gotten up) noticed us leaving and accosted us and charged us the $3 rip-off fee for sleeping there.

Our plan now was to go to Mexico to humor Sally, who had been pestering us continually to take her there so she could buy all sorts of cheap clothes with my money. So we drove all the long way down to the border, planning to tell the nice officials at the gate that we were only going about 30 miles inside to find a beach and spend nice American dollars for Indian beadwork and other native items, and so we don't need a passport to go only a short way in.

We saw two officials at the border. The US official smiled and said, "See that long line of people over there? They have been turned back because their hair was too long. Good luck." The Mexican official gave us a xenophobic look and said, pointing to me, "This man cannot go; his hair too long." Then he hissed directions at us to turn around. We left, gnashing our teeth and rending our garments; I cast ashes on my hair as a penance and scratched my face with my nails until it bled, crying, "Wherefore was I to this keen mockery born?" (Well, maybe that was an exaggeration.)

As soon as we had turned around and proceeded to leave the border area, the car began making funny flapping noises. Tom feared that something might be drastically wrong with it, so as soon as we got into San Diego, he dropped Sally and me off at Torrey Pines State Beach while he went off to find a gas station that could tell him what was happening.

Tom did not return for five whole hours. Sally and I had been worried that maybe he had been captured by locals, or spirited off by some nymph or sylph of the mountains who had sealed him up in a tree, or maybe he had even lost his way. But it turned out that the problem with the car was with the universal joint, and to replace it, Tom had to run all over town to find a new one and someone to install it.

After that traumatic quest, Tom stayed around the beach and splashed and played in the warm water, thoroughly content with life and its exigencies. Then we climbed up a nearby set of hills to watch the sunset, a truly impressive sight. While we were thus watching, we met a guy and a girl who asked us if we could give them a ride into town. We said sure, if they in turn would tell us where there was a good restaurant. It turned out that the guy (named Martin) was a student from Basel, Switzerland, visiting his girlfriend (originally from Switzerland and named something or other) in San Diego. We gave them a ride all the way home and took their advice by eating at the Hamburger House, a reputable establishment where we were waited upon by one Marge, who Tom was sufficiently captivated by for him to leave an exceptionally large tip. That Tom. What he won't do.

We now decided to sneak back into Doheny State Beach and leave before the ranger got up the next morning. But first we bought some beer in Laguna Beach and went onto a side street to drink some of it and wait for Doheny's ranger to close up shop.

While approaching Doheny at a time when we thought it was reasonable to deduce that the ranger had left, we were accosted by a cop car with flashing lights. It contained two more Orange County sheriffs, not the same ones who had harassed us yesterday, but just as cold and menacing. They said to Tom, kid, whaddya think you're doing with only one taillight, huh, pointing to the taillight that had been disconnected accidentally because we had so much stuff in the trunk. They told us that in these parts, this was against the Law.

Then they illegally searched our car, finding the beer and one empty beer can, which they said was wrong because you're not supposed to carry an "open container" in the car, a rule that lends itself quite well to arbitrary harassment. Then they quite illegally searched us, finding nothing, naturally, because Sally had hidden her grass well in the car.

This second harassment was too much for us and we could not take it. We took one cop and threw scalding water over his feet and cast guts and offal upon him, after which we nearly hammered the soul from his body and threw him on a train to Mexicali where he would be sold to a drug cartel for ransom. We threw the other cop into a dry gulch, where his lungs were choked and blood spurted from under his nails and he perished in the mud like a mangled donkey. (Or perhaps I made this all up as a literary device.)

We snuck back into Doheny and slept restlessly. Sally didn't actually sleep at all—she wandered around the beach by herself and went to a gas station where she ran into two cops and rapped with them for a long time, telling them (politely) what she thought of local police procedures.

Wednesday, September 16, 1970

"*As soon as fayre Aurora from the deawy bed of aged Tithone gan her selfe to reare,*" we snuck out of Doheny without paying and left for home. We could not go faster than 55 mph or the car would fall apart, which is why we made it no further than to Holbrook, Arizona, by nightfall. We slept at a rest stop along the freeway.

Thursday, September 17, 1970

We decided not to drive to Santa Fe to pick up Ozone because the Mustang was driving poorly and it was out of our way and our time was getting shorter and he probably wouldn't have been there anyway because the guy was somewhat on the shiftless side. We drove all the way to Foss Reservoir, Oklahoma, where we once again bedded down.

Friday, September 18, 1970

Tom drove all day and all night and we arrived in Columbus, Ohio, at 11:00 a.m. Saturday morning, breaking exactly even money-wise.

And that was the end of The Long Haul. I returned to university classes at Ohio State and my job at Riverside Methodist Hospital in Columbus. In a few years, I graduated with a degree in journalism, got some work experience in the Ohio State University Libraries, then moved to Chicago to get a master's degree at the University of Chicago Graduate Library School.

For many years, these narratives sat in a box in the basement, mostly forgotten. Now they have been unearthed and restored, offering a glimpse of people and places from the past.

What a long, strange trip it's been.

Printed in the USA
CPSIA information can be obtained
at www.ICGtesting.com
CBHW021941010624
9310CB00004B/95